THE COMPLETE HUNTER™

WATERFOWL HUNTING

Ducks and Geese of North America

NICK SMITH

Creative Publishing
international

www.creativepub.com

Dedication

To my mother and father, who either through a plethora of educational outings or adventures to pursue waterfowl, taught me the true joys of wildlife biology and hunting.

And to my younger brother, Will. Without his personality and diehard wingshooting spirit, I wouldn't have the hunting partner I have today.

Acknowledgments

Heartfelt thanks go to friends and fellow outdoor writers who have shared much of themselves with me in the wonderful world of waterfowling. It's been through their camaraderie and laughter that I have learned not to take this game so seriously.

NICK SMITH has been published in many prestigious outdoor magazines, such as *American Angler, Outdoors Magazine,* and *Fur-Fish-Game.* He owns and operates Vermont Outdoor Connections Guide Service, which specializes in quality duck and goose hunting adventures. Nick lives in Bomoseen, Vermont.

Creative Publishing international

Copyright © 2006 by Creative Publishing international, Inc.
18705 Lake Drive East
Chanhassen, MN 55317
1-800-328-3895
www.creativepub.com

President/CEO: Ken Fund
Vice President/Retail Sales & Marketing: Kevin Haas
Executive Editor, Outdoor Group: Barbara Harold
Creative Director: Brad Springer
Book Designer: Kari Johnston
Production Manager: Laura Hokkanen

Printed in China

10 9 8 7 6 5 4 3 2 1

WATERFOWL HUNTING
by Nick Smith

Cover Photo: © Creative Publishing international, Inc.

Contributing Photographers: Tricia Bergstue, John R. Ford, Michael H. Francis, Michael Furtman, Eric J. Hansen, Donald M. Jones, Gary Kramer, William H. Mullins, Dusan Smetana, Will Smith, Bill Vinje

Contributing Manufacturers: Benelli USA, Carlson Championship Calls, LLC, Cass Creek Game Calls, Flambeau Outdoors, Gooseview Industries, Haydel's Game Calls, Inc., Hunter's Specialties, Knight & Hale Game Calls, Open Zone, Inc., Renzo's Decoys, Wing Wavers, Inc.

Library of Congress Cataloging-in-Publication Data

Smith, Nick.
  Waterfowl hunting : ducks and geese of North America / Nick Smith.
       p. cm. -- (The complete hunter series)
    Includes index.
    ISBN 1-58923-237-2 (hard cover)
    1. Waterfowl shooting--North America. I. Title. II. Complete hunter (Creative Publishing international, Inc.)
     SK331.S545 2006
     799.2'44'097--dc22
                                    2005023738

WATERFOWL HUNTING

CONTENTS

Introduction

Even before I began writing this book, I spent hours in reflection. It was important to me that the reader be exposed to many of the common aspects of waterfowling, such as decoying and calling, but also to some less-covered topics. There are many books that touch on a particular aspect of this glorious sport. Shooting, calling and camouflage have all had their fair share of ink, though few publications seem to cover some of the important ones. It is my hope this book does just that.

Touching on my years of experience owning and operating Vermont Outdoor Connections Guide Service, I wrote this book with the intention of leaving a thick residue of duck- and goose-hunting tricks and techniques that the average hunter could employ for instant results. Techniques and strategies that I have spent years examining and perfecting are outlined here.

As you peruse the pages, you will see that the sections aren't only filled with technical hunting tips and strategies, but they also contain a basic understanding of waterfowl biology. This standard set of observations must be absorbed before any hunter goes afield.

Beyond pre-hunt biology, various chapters touch on critical aspects that make our sport so intriguing. From shotgun mechanics and techniques to the know-how involved with decoys, there is a nuts-and-bolts area for everyone.

Lastly, this book isn't meant to be read once and stowed on a dusty bookshelf. It's my hope that it becomes a reference source, used again and again. It's taken me years to explore the hunting techniques and strategies discussed here. Take advantage of the trials and tribulations that I had to endure. Remembering many unfortunate moments brought on by bad planning and poor technique is difficult. Bask in my mistakes and take from them the knowledge that they have given me.

Remember also, keeping a concerned eye on wetland protection, hunting and conservation efforts, we as hunters can be proud of our involvement and investment in this great sport.

May the wind be at your back and mallards under your brim.

CHAPTER ONE

Life Cycle of Waterfowl

Waterfowl species, by nature, are seasonal creatures. Just gaze at an autumn sky and you may see strings of these game birds en route to a warmer destination. Like having an internal clock, all waterfowl seem to use a seasonal schedule to live a successful life. While duck and goose behavior may seem similar, the nuances of their habits are quite different. Even within the duck species, puddlers and divers are differentiated by variations in plumage, vocalization, flight pattern and anatomical structure.

FOOD & FEEDING HABITS

The general diet of waterfowl varies with species, weather and geographic location. In general, ducks and geese will key in on a specific food or crop that is available during a particular season. In mid- to late spring, fresh shoots, tubers, grasses, insects, snails and fish are utilized. In the fall and winter, this can mean farm crops, such as corn, rice, grains and cultivated vegetables; it can also mean natural selections, such as acorns, seeds and any remaining grass.

Aquatic insects and vegetation sources are also very important during most of the year. Many species of aquatic macrophytes (aquatic plants), such as smart weed, wigeon grass, wild celery, water lily and bulrush seeds, play important roles in a duck's diet when months away from the fall harvest.

Besides the actual food consumed, the manner in which ducks and geese feed can differ drastically from species to species. Some may dive several feet (meters) to feed, while others may simply bob down and feed in the subsurface or bottom of shallower pools.

DUCKS

In the spring, flocks of mating pairs return north from their southern winter retreats to locate a lake, river or wetland appropriate for conceiving and raising their broods. Consequently, most waterfowl breeding is done in the northern United States and Canada, where the majority of the species spend their spring and summer months. Soon after breeding, the drake molts, losing all distinguishable feathers, making him closely resemble the hen. The hen molts much later, once her brood is almost fully grown. Employing internal homing instincts, many return to the original bodies of water where they were hatched.

Some believed that ducks mate for life. However, studies now show that this isn't entirely true. The best evidence depicting mating habits can be seen in courtship flights. This is when several males locate and target a single female, flying around her and displaying themselves simultaneously. While it's quite possible for a pair to mate for life, mortality rates from natural predation, disease, drought and hunting, tend to prove otherwise.

Following copulation, the hen locates a suitable nest site, which may range from a dry hummock to a thick, brushy or grassy patch to a hollowed tree,

and begins assembling a nest. Each location is species specific, and ducks don't simply choose a location on a whim.

Once a suitable and safe location is found, the hen lays 4 to 12 eggs at a rate of one egg each day. As the clutch nears completion, the hen plucks a few breast feathers to line the nest and cushion the eggs, also creating added insulation. Individual eggs in a clutch usually hatch within 5 to 6 hours of each other. Some species' new chicks even enter the water only hours later.

If the vulnerable and fragile chicks survive their first 4 to 6 weeks of life, they produce their first pre-adult flight feathers and learn to fly. Now fledglings, their risk of being eaten by predators drops dramatically. Water predators include large game fish, such as northern pike, largemouth bass and trout; land predators include skunks, raccoons, birds and foxes.

In the early summer, the chicks lose their yellow or gray down (depending on species) and develop feather coloration similar to their mother's. These fledglings spend almost the entire summer displaying those female markings, and consequently are difficult to identify.

As summer progresses to early autumn, drakes begin to grow their more colorful plumage and begin their eclipse phase. Much like the spring molting of the adult drake, young males slowly develop the coloration hunters come to rely on for identification in future months.

Depending on the species and its particular flyway, the autumn migration southward can begin as early as the first week in August and last until January. Feeding and resting in their southern zones, the cycle begins again in a few months.

Puddle Ducks

With the least number of ducks being of the "puddle" variety, this group is far easier for the hunter to identify. Here are a few tips:

• With large wings, these species are able to lift vertically from the surface, unlike their faster and smaller-winged cousins, the divers.

• Utilizing their larger wing structure, puddle ducks employ fewer wing beats per second and give the illusion of flying slower than other species, except for the teal species, which are much closer in size to divers than most puddle ducks.

• Puddlers are more suited to land travel, with legs positioned closer to the center of the body. And, coupled with smaller feet, balance is much greater.

• The majority of puddler vocalizations are coarse and gravelly clucking sounds, with lots of quacking. Except for pintails, wigeons and wood ducks, very little whistling is done by this group.

• Puddlers rarely feed in deep-water environments, but rather rely on shallow pools and wetlands. The technique they employ is called dabbling, lifting their rear toward the sky and simply bobbing down to feed. Hence their other nickname, "dabblers."

• Their diet is usually more vegetarian than that of divers, with a propensity for not only aquatic plants, but also for all farm crops. Despite their appetite for vegetation, they will also eat insects, snails, tadpoles and occasionally small fish.

• Because they eat mainly plant matter, puddler meat is much milder than that of the diver species, and favored by most sportsmen.

• Many males are very colorful but some, such as the gadwall, are quite drab.

Diver Ducks

Diver species make up the second largest of the overall duck population (after mallards), but are some of the least known, or easily confused.

- With their smaller wings, divers are forced to run a short way to gain enough power to lift into the air.

- Divers are better suited for deeper aquatic environments, with their legs positioned at the rear of their body. They also have much larger feet than puddle ducks. This physical combination affords the duck the ability to dive to depths exceeding 20 feet (6.1 m).

- The majority of diver vocalization is in the form of whistles. While this can vary greatly by species, the overall language resembles chirps, whistles and hoarse quacks or growls.

- Their diet is mainly protein—fish, crayfish, clams, snails and some aquatic vegetation. This makes their meat have a gamy taste and only a few species are suitable table fare. One tip: avoid the mergansers for your menu!

- Divers display plumage with very few color or pattern combinations. While many have been noted to have an interesting or a visually pleasing design, there is little variation, and most simply have a barred pattern mixed with solid natural colors.

GEESE

Beginning in early spring, lifelong mating pairs begin migration to their northernmost breeding grounds to conceive and raise their brood together. Unlike ducks, the male (or gander) remains with the female throughout her incubation period and, upon hatching, aids in the chicks' development.

In search of a nesting site, geese are more particular and won't simply settle for a small stream or puddle. Being much larger birds, nesting sites are on average much larger in overall area. Backwaters of lakes or ponds afford geese superior protection from predation, as well as being a valued food source for chicks (or goslings).

In their more northern reaches, geese use large tracts of grassland (tundra) and simply rely on the aid of a large population to ensure life. Little protection is afforded, as nesting options are limited.

Nest building is quite similar to that of many ducks, as they employ the same techniques and use the same mud, reeds and other materials. However, goose nests are usually placed on elevated portions of land, if not assembled on the artic

grasslands. Hummocks, muskrat huts and beaver lodges or dams are common foundations. While not only protecting the eggs and chicks from common seasonal floods, the elevated platforms also afford the parents a 360-degree view of approaching danger.

Following copulation, 4 to 10 eggs are laid and incubated by the female for one month. It takes the chicks 1½ to 2 days to completely hatch. The young travel, feed and socialize with their parents on a daily basis.

Between 40 and 70 days of age, the chicks attain their first flight feathers and become fledglings. Never bearing an eclipse stage, the fledglings look almost identical to both parents. Later summer molting does little to change their overall appearance.

Upon reaching their final stage of maturity, the last of their grayish white down falls out with the appearance of their adult feathers. They continue to stay with the home flock until locating mates during their first autumn.

CHAPTER TWO

Puddle Duck Species

For centuries, ducks have been a source of fascination for hunters and nonhunters alike. But with so many duck species, learning to identify them and understand their behavior is a challenge, even to those who have spent a lifetime studying them.

Here are four general tips to help identify a puddler:

• Tipping up, or dabbling, is the usual puddle duck feeding method.

• Legs positioned near the center of the body give a puddler good balance, so it can easily walk and feed on land.

• Colored wing patches are present on most puddlers. Most have a patch, called a speculum, on the wing's trailing edge, which is usually iridescent.

• Puddle ducks commonly feed in harvested crop fields. The birds fly in to feed in the morning, fly back to the water to rest in midday, then return to the feeding fields in late afternoon. In cold weather, they may make several feeding flights during the day.

The detailed range maps in this chapter show you exactly where to find each species. You'll see where they breed and spend the summer, and where they winter. A color key for the range maps is shown below.

Key to Duck Range Maps

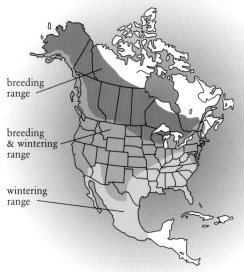

breeding range

breeding & wintering range

wintering range

Mallard

The most common and most commonly pursued species, mallards are also considered one of the most social, often using their calls to lure other ducks. Averaging 2½ to 3½ pounds (1.12 to 1.58 kg) and more than 20 inches (50.8 cm) long, they are by far one of the largest and hardiest puddle species. Beginning their migration in late October through December, hunting opportunities can seem limited when local populations are scarce. Large flocks seek a well-used crop field and a small patch of open water nearby when severe weather hits. Knowing that they feed mainly on farm crops such as corn, soybean and grains during their migration, locating flocks can seem easy. With drakes sporting an iridescent green head, they are one of the most easily recognized species. The drake has a white neck ring and a rusty-colored breast. The belly and sides are silvery white; the back, gray. The hen (or susie) is mottled brown overall, with a lighter belly and darker back. Her bill is orange with black blotches. Both sexes have orange legs and feet, and a blue-violet speculum with white margins.

Northern Pintail

A rarity for eastern hunters, the pintail is a beautiful species. Nicknamed "sprig" after its easily identifiable long tail, drakes can measure more than 25 inches (63.5 cm) and weigh 2½ to 3 pounds (1.12 to 1.35 kg). Hens are slightly shorter and lighter. Males sport a chocolate-colored head, gray/black barred sides and tri-colored wings of black, gray and white. The speculum is green. Hens are dull in comparison with mottled brown sides and a tan head. Wings are multi-colored, yet sport a brownish majority, including the speculum. Much like the mallard's diet, pintails eat all the major farm crops as well as aquatic vegetation. Techniques for hunting are similar to those used for mallards, with the only difference being the option to use a pintail whistle call to imitate the males. Hens sound almost identical to hen mallards. While purchasing pintail decoys isn't entirely necessary for hunting, adding a few to a half dozen to any spread will add color and realism.

American Black Duck

Much more difficult to identify, this duck looks much like a hen mallard, but with a darker, almost black, coloration. The speculum is blue with black edges, in contrast to the white-edged speculum on the mallard. Both males and females can seem identical, yet the greenish yellow bill color of the male versus the dark or slightly orange coloration of the female are sure distinguishers. Weighing 2 to 3½ pounds (0.9 to 1.58 kg) and measuring 20 inches (50.8 cm) long, they both closely resemble the size of the mallard. Popularly hunted in the mid-Atlantic states, they frequent both coastal and freshwater wetland environments. Forage for the black duck can seem much like that of the mallard, excluding their coastal diet of crustaceans. Hunting techniques are very similar to those used with mallards, as they can be easily attracted with mallard calls and decoys. Locating larger waterways in early to mid-October gives the waterfowler ample hunting opportunities. As the season progresses, blacks mix with flocks of mallards and great hunting opportunities can be expected anywhere mallards are found.

Gadwall

Both males and females weigh 1½ to 2½ pounds (0.68 to 1.12 kg) and measure 18 to 20 inches (45.7 to 50.8 cm). With both presenting brownish mottled feathers, identification can be difficult. But subtle traits make it possible. Males display barred, brown-and-black sides, while hens display the common brownish tan feathers, much like a female mallard. A drake gadwall has a much darker head than the female, as well as a blackish bill. The speculum is white on both sexes, framed by black and brown feathers. Gadwalls prefer aquatic plants and stems such as coontail, wigeon grass and musk grass. For northern hunters, locating gadwalls can be difficult, as they begin their migration in early to mid-September and arrive at their wintering grounds in late October or early November. Hunting techniques for gadwalls can be closely compared with late-season black or mallard methods. Locating active potholes and using mallard calls and decoys are proven choices. While gadwall decoys are available, a flock of mallard hen decoys will suffice perfectly.

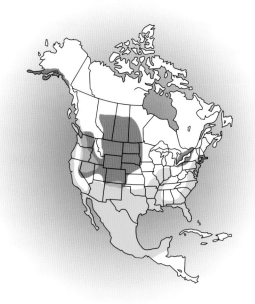

American Wigeon

Easily identifiable, the drake has a tri-colored body of brown, white and black, with a green streak running from the eye down the back of the neck. It also has a white splash on the top of the head. The hen displays the same tri-colored body, but with more of a buff color, rather than white. There is no white on the top of the hen's head. Primarily a western species, few are found in the East. Hunting techniques for the wigeon (also known as the "baldpate") are the same as for mallards, with the majority lured to wigeon or mallard decoys with mallard hen calls. To ensure success, hunt during the early season, as migration can start as early as mid-August and into September.

Wood Duck

Nearly extinct during the early 1920s, due to habitat loss, the wood duck is known as one of the greatest wildlife management success stories in history. Today, the wood duck is quite common in much of North America. Unlike many other puddlers, wood ducks predominantly feed on woodland plants such as acorns, hickory nuts, seeds and, when available, corn. Measuring 15 to 18 inches (38.1 to 45.7 cm) and weighing around 2 pounds (0.9 kg), they are one of the smaller puddle species. Though, with males sporting lemon-colored flank feathers, green-and-white heads, dark green crests and multi-colored bills, they are one of the easiest to identify. Hens are much more drab in comparison, with the majority of their plumage a grayish brown, yet also displaying a crest. Both sexes have a blue speculum, and the legs and feet are yellow, though the color is duller in hens. Hunting techniques can seem immensely different from those for many puddle ducks, as this species never quacks, but rather whistles to communicate. Hunters harvest many "woodies" while jump-shooting creeks or hidden ponds, while others use wood duck decoys and whistles to lure them.

Blue-Winged Teal

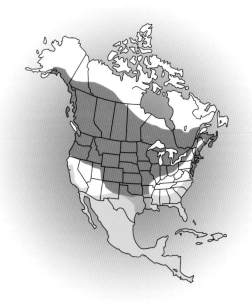

The second smallest of the puddle species, the blue-winged teal is an aerial acrobat, dipping and diving like a bat while in flight. Weighing ½ to 1 pound (0.23 to 0.45 kg) and measuring 13 to 15 inches (33 to 38.1 cm) long, teals make tiny targets. Identification is relatively simple, with males displaying an almost polka-dot look, a grayish head and white stripe in front of the eye. Hens are a dull mottled brown, yet both have brilliant blue speculum feathers. Common diets consist of aquatic plants such as coontail, musk grass and duckweed. Hunting methods are no different than for the majority of puddle duck species, with the majority of hunters using nasally teal quacks and whistle calls.

Green-Winged Teal

This smallest of the puddle species weighs in at approximately ½ to ¾ pound (0.23 to 0.34 kg) and measures 13 to 15 inches (33 to 38.1 cm). The green-winged is more distinguishable than its blue-winged cousin. Males sport a rust-colored head with a green slash slightly above and surrounding the eye, and a green speculum. Barred, gray-and-black sides and light-brown wings make it easy to identify. Hens are almost identical to hen blue-wings, but have a slightly lighter bill. Both have emerald-colored speculum feathers. Their diet is similar to that of the blue-wings, with aquatic plants being the main staple. Hunting techniques are identical to the blue-winged, with both species eagerly coming to all puddle decoys and most puddle calls. While not always a challenge to decoy or call, both male and female will test even the most polished wingshooter with their unequaled flying abilities.

Cinnamon Teal

The cinnamon teal resides in the western and southwestern United States, as well as in some southeastern states and Mexico. Weighing ½ to 1 pound (0.23 to 0.45 kg) and measuring 14 to 17 inches (35.5 to 43.2 cm) long, it displays the common body size of all teal species. An easy species to identify, the cinnamon drake sports a beautiful cinnamon-colored body, tri-colored wings (tan, black, buff) and an iridescent green speculum. Females display the expected dull brown and tan coloration, almost identical to the blue-winged and green-winged teal. Large bill size and black coloring are the only ways to truly identify the cinnamon hen from other hen teals. Their diet is similar to that of other teal species, with bulrush seeds, pondweed leaves and some mollusks being the staple ingredients. Migration is quite early, with most birds beginning in late August, and ultimately arriving in late November in South America to escape winter temperatures. Hunting methods are exactly the same as for many puddle species, as most cinnamons are killed while hunters are in pursuit of other species.

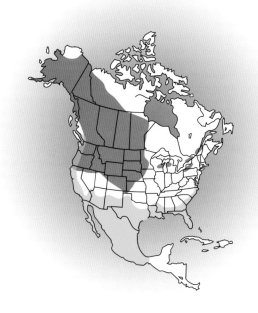

Northern Shoveler

With drakes sporting a green head, much like the mallard, a white chest, chocolate sides and green speculum, identification is easy. Females are dull brown, with body coloration much like a hen mallard. The wide shovel-like bill can be seen in both sexes. Weighing in at 1½ to 2 pounds (0.68 to 0.9 kg) and measuring 17 to 20 inches (43.2 to 50.8 cm) long, it's one of the larger puddle species. Shovelers feed by a method unique to their species: using their large bill to filter plankton from the water and to skim the surface of mud for insects and other invertebrates. Feasting mainly on animal life, their meat has a strong, gamy taste. Beginning their migration in early September, they arrive in the southern United States and Mexico in late November. Hunting techniques are similar to those of other puddle styles, with the majority harvested incidentally by hunters chasing mallards and gadwalls.

CHAPTER THREE

Diver Duck Species

lying low over the water in tight flocks is typical behavior among most diver species. In flight, divers can often be distinguished from puddlers by their shorter, faster wingbeat.

Here are four more general tips to help identify a diver:

• Running on the water helps divers gain enough speed for take-off. Their small wings provide less lift than those of puddlers.

• Large feet and legs positioned far back on the body account for the diving ability of these ducks.

• White to dark gray wing patches are found on most diving duck species.

• Diving ducks plunge well beneath the surface to feed.

The detailed range maps in this chapter show you exactly where to find each species. You'll see where they breed and spend the summer, and where they winter. A color key for the range maps is shown below.

Key to Duck Range Maps

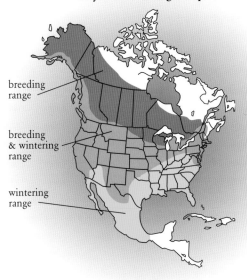

breeding range

breeding & wintering range

wintering range

Canvasback

Said by many to be the most sought after diver species, the canvasback is not only beautiful to look at, but also easily identifiable. Drakes sport a rust-colored head, black chest and white body. Their profile is much sleeker than most species', with a long black beak and sloping head. Hens display a mottled white-and-tan body, with an almost-solid-tan chest and head. Weighing approximately 3 to 3½ pounds (1.35 to 1.58 kg) and measuring 18 to 22 inches (45.7 to 55.9 cm), they are a large bird. Their diet consists of a variety of staples including wild celery, sago pondweed, bulrush seeds, mollusks, crustaceans and fish. Despite their propensity for fish, the balance of vegetation in their diet makes their meat quite pleasing to the palate. Beginning their migration in late September, they may spend several weeks on large bodies of water while en route. Their migration ends in January when reaching the Gulf Coast states and Mexico. Hunting techniques used to consistently bag canvasbacks are large diver decoy spreads on lakes and saltwater estuaries, along with most diver calls.

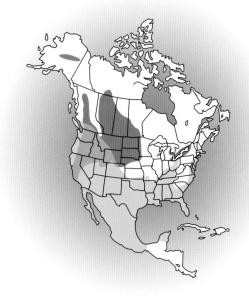

Redhead

Almost identical in appearance to the canvasback, the redhead can be easily misidentified. With drakes sporting many of the same features as the drake canvasback, the only major differences can be seen along the drake's sides, which are a barred white and black, instead of the pure white coloration. The redhead also has a shorter blue bill, which joins the face in a less streamlined appearance. Females are of the same general shape, but with an overall tan or brownish color. Weighing approximately 2 to 2¾ pounds (0.9 to 1.24 kg) and measuring 18 to 22 inches (45.7 to 55.9 cm), it can quite easily be mistaken for the canvasback.

Like their canvasback cousins, redheads feed primarily on vegetation with only a small portion of their diet consisting of fish and mollusks. Hunting methods are the same as for the canvasback, with large bodies of water and strings of decoys being the ace in the hole.

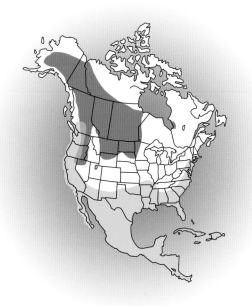

Lesser Scaup

The lesser scaup is commonly known as the blue-bill. It is slightly smaller than the greater scaup, and perhaps less colorful. Drakes sport a black head and chest, bluish bill and white-and-black mottled back and sides. Females sport a brownish head and chest, with whitish brown sides, black tail and back. The female also has a whitish blotch around her bill, making identification much easier than with most female duck species. Both sexes sport a long, white speculum. Weighing 2 to 2½ pounds (0.9 to 1.12 kg) and measuring 15 to 18 inches (38.1 to 45.7 cm), it's an average-size diver. The bluebill's diet is made up of mostly mollusks, aquatic invertebrates, clams and snails, but the ducks also feed on aquatic vegetation such as wild celery and wigeon grass. Migration begins in late September with the majority of the flocks arriving in late October through December. Hunting techniques are the same as for many other diver species, with the lesser scaup being one of the easiest species to decoy. Diver calls are also an asset.

Greater Scaup

Weighing 2½ to 3 pounds (1.12 to 1.35 kg), and measuring 16 to 18 inches (40.6 to 45.7 cm) long, the greater scaup is not only slightly larger than the lesser, but also currently has a larger population. The drake sports a dark green to nearly black head, white sides and a barred, black-and-gray back. Hens display a barred, mottled tan-and-black back, with a black head. Like the lesser hen, this hen also has a blotch of white around her bill. Both sexes sport a white speculum. The greater's diet is based primarily on clams, pondweeds and wild celery. Migration begins in September, with birds reaching the wintering grounds by October. The Great Lakes, coastal estuaries and Gulf Coast states routinely harbor the wintering fowl. Hunting techniques are the same as for the lesser, with only small modifications in the decoy colorations.

Ring-Necked Duck

This is an average-size, mild-tasting duck. It is also known as a "ringneck," and demonstrates habits more like a puddle species. Preferring to feed on pondweed, duckweed, coontail and other aquatic vegetation, ringnecks feed predominantly in shallow pools, ponds and marshes. It weighs 1½ to 2 pounds (0.68 to 0.9 kg) and measures 16 to 19 inches (40.6 to 48.3 cm). Sporting a black head and chest and grayish white sides, the ringneck at a quick glance can be mistaken for a lesser scaup. At closer inspection, the lack of barring and coloration on the male's sides is a solid identifier. Hens display a brown mottled coloration over their entire body. Both sexes have a white band across their bill. Migration begins in mid-October and ends in late November through early December. Successful hunting techniques are the same as with other divers.

Bufflehead

A small diving species, the bufflehead weighs ¾ to 1 pound (0.34 to 0.45 kg) and measures approximately 14 inches (35.5 cm) long. Males sport white sides and breast, and a black head and back. Identification can be easy, as the blotch of white on the upper side and back of the head is a distinguishing feature. Females are dull in color, with a white breast, smoky-colored sides and a black head and back. The white blotch on the head is much smaller on the females and sits under the eye. Their general diet is fish and aquatic invertebrates, with some vegetation also regularly consumed. Migration begins much later than most species, as they begin in mid-October and reach their wintering grounds in the continental United States and Mexico in December. Hunting techniques employ the same strategies as with all divers, yet this species isn't nearly as sought after, as the meat has a fishy flavor.

Common Goldeneye

A strong-tasting bird, the common goldeneye (or "whistler") weighs approximately 3 to 3½ pounds (1.35 to 1.58 kg) and measures 16 to 18 inches (40.6 to 45.7 cm). The coloration is in keeping with the black and white diver pattern—the males can be identified by their black head with greenish sheen and a white dot. Males also show a white chest and sides, and striped black-and-white wings. Females are a duller smoky color, and both have a brilliant golden eye. Favoring lakes and large waterways, their diet is based primarily on fish, including only some vegetation. One of the last to leave their breeding grounds, goldeneyes stay until the water freezes and eventually arrive in the northern United States to winter by late November. Hunting methods are similar to those for other divers, with the only difference being decoy placement, which generally requires more decoys per spread and usually in a fishhook pattern.

Barrow's Goldeneye

The Barrow's weighs just 1½ to 2 pounds (0.68 to 0.9 kg) and measures 15 to 16 inches (38.1 to 40.6 cm). Males are very similar in coloration to the common, but instead of a white blotch on the cheek area, a line of teardrop shape is present and the head has a purple sheen. A black band running from the back and separating the breast from the side is also a visual difference. Hens have a more defined head and breast line, with a much darker head and shorter, yellow-and-black bill. Migration is similar to the common, with the Barrow's leaving earlier and arriving as early as late October. The Barrow's diet is almost identical to the common and, consequently, they are found in the same habitats and are hunted identically.

Ruddy Duck

Even smaller than the Barrow's, the ruddy weighs ¾ to 1 pound (0.34 to 0.45 kg) and measures 14 to 16 inches (35.5 to 40.6 cm). Males display near-stiff tail feathers, chestnut body, black-and-white head and blue bill. They look nothing like any other species. Females can be confused with hens of some puddle ducks, as they are commonly dull brown or tan and sport that puddle duck-like dark bill. Feeding mainly on aquatic vegetation such as wigeon grass, bulrush seeds and pondweed, their meat is mild. Migration begins in September with most birds reaching the wintering grounds in the south by December. Hunting methods will seem opposite of those for most diver species, as these ducks feed in water only 2 to 8 or 9 feet (0.61 to 2.44 or 2.74 m) deep. Puddler hunting methods must be employed, as these birds rarely ever reach large tracts of open water.

Harlequin

With populations in very low numbers, hunting has been stopped almost completely for this species. Weighing 1¼ to 1½ pounds (0.56 to 0.68 kg) and measuring 14 to 17 inches (35.5 to 43.2 cm) long, they are smaller than the average diver. Males sport blue-gray plumage, chestnut sides, and many distinguishing white slashes and blotches. The hen is colored more like a female wood duck; only one white blotch can be found on her head. Their diet is similar to that of other sea ducks, with crustaceans, mollusks and fish comprising the majority. While spending a great deal of time around the ocean, harlequins also frequent fresh-water environments. Migration begins in mid-September and concludes when they reach the sea coast.

Common Merganser

Weighing approximately 3½ to 4¼ pounds (1.58 to 2.03 kg) and measuring 23 to 25 inches (58.4 to 63.5 cm), it's a much larger bird than the hooded, and only second in size to the largest diver species, the common eider. Both hen and drake are easy to identify, with the drake sporting a green head with no crest, black back, and white sides and chest. The hen has a rust-colored head, with a noticeable crest, and a gray chest, back and sides. Feeding primarily on fish, the common merganser has been known to decimate schools of baitfish, as well as hurt local trout populations through flock hunting practices. A hearty species, it is one of the last ducks to begin migration, and many never leave, relying on open rivers and channels to feed throughout the winter. Again, hunting is minimal, as most are taken incidentally or by anglers trying to restore a fishery.

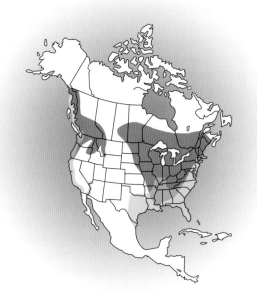

Hooded Merganser

Drakes sport large crests or "hoods" in white and black, white breasts, barred chestnut sides and white-and-black wings. Hens also have hoods, but display a mud-color, gray breast and white-and-black wings. Weighing 1½ to 2 pounds (0.68 to 0.9 kg) and measuring 15 to 17 inches (38.1 to 43.2 cm), they are close in size to the Barrow's goldeneye. With their diet mainly based on amphibians, crustaceans and fish, their meat isn't suitable table fare. Migration begins in mid-October and ends by November when birds arrive in the Southeast. Few hunters target any merganser species and most are harvested incidentally, or by fly-tiers.

King Eider

The king eider drake displays one of the most beautiful head pieces of all waterfowl. A patch of yellow and black feathers surround the bill, while a baby-blue color covers the top and back of the head and neck. A whitish green fills the void around the eye and cheek. The chest is a creamy color with a few speckles in the front, and a black back and sides. White breaks up the black on the rump and a line runs under the wings. Females are a golden chestnut color, with a black and brown pattern on their body. The diet of this sea duck is based primarily on invertebrates with very few fish. Being equipped to feed much deeper than the common eider, they have been documented diving more than 150 feet (45.7 m) at a time. Migration begins as early as July or August and they arrive in their wintering grounds between September and December. Their wintering areas are the same as for the common eider, as are the methods used to pursue them.

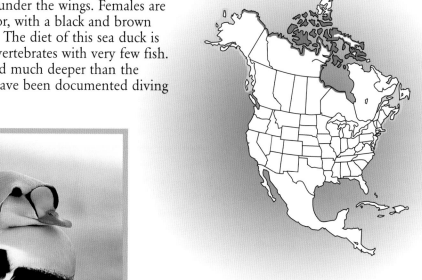

Common Eider

The largest of all North American ducks, the common eider weighs approximately 6 to 6½ pounds (2.7 to 2.9 kg) and measures 25 to 26 inches (63.5 to 66 cm). Males sport a white back, black sides, white-and-black head streaked with white, and a yellowish nape. Hens are an overall dull brown, displaying a black and tan pattern on their body. Both display long, sloping bills. A sea duck, their diet is based on crustaceans, mollusks and fish. While generally feeding in shallow waters, they have been known to dive as deep as 50 or 60 feet (15.24 to 18.29 m) in search of food. Migration

begins in mid-September, with the majority of the birds reaching open seas of western Alaska or eastern Canada by mid-October or early November. Hunting for these or any sea duck isn't for the faint of heart. Most hunting is done by driving several miles from shore with converted lobster boats and setting large lines of decoys with smaller hunting vessels. If hunting pressure has been minimal, hunters can also set up off from rocky points closer to land.

Long-Tailed

Not known by many North American sportsmen because of restricted hunting opportunities, the long-tailed or "oldsquaw" is actually one of the most common ducks worldwide. Weighing 2 to 2½ pounds (0.9 to 1.12 kg) and measuring 19 to 23 inches (48.3 to 58.4 cm), including their long tail, they are of average size. This is the only duck to have four distinctly different plumages depending on season. The color phase that hunters commonly see is when the autumn male specimen has a dark brown back and sides, gray wing patches, white chest and a white, black, brown and tan head, displayed in a half-moon pattern. This duck carries a long, dark brown tail. Female coloration resembles that of juvenile penguins with a mottled brown-and-gray back and mottled brown-and-white sides. Their diet consists of mollusks, crustaceans, fish and insect larvae. Migration begins in early September and ends in November or early December, when reaching coastal bays along the Atlantic and Pacific seaboard. Hunting methods are similar to those for other sea species, with regular success found in deep water.

White-Winged Scoter

A seafaring species, it measures 20 to 23 inches (50.8 to 58.4 cm) and weighs 2½ to 3½ pounds (1.12 to 1.58 kg). It closely resembles the other scoter species. Drakes sport a black body, dark brown sides and white eye slashed with a white streak. Females are almost completely black, with smaller hints of white underneath each wing. Their diets include mostly shelled organisms such as crabs, mollusks, barnacles and mussels. Not shallow-water feeders, white-winged scoters have been known to dive to depths of 90 feet (27.4 m) to feed. Migration begins in late September, and ends in December or January when the birds have reached the Great Lakes, Atlantic coast or Texas panhandle. Hunting techniques are the same as for other sea ducks.

Surf Scoter

Appearing much like the white-winged, the female is slightly lighter and much smaller, weighing approximately 1½ to 2½ pounds (0.68 to 1.12 kg) and measuring 17 to 21 inches (43.2 to 53.3 cm) long. The male is about the same general size, with a broader bill and a white patch on forehead and nape. The diet is also similar to that of the white-winged, with the bulk of it being mollusks, crustaceans, wigeon grass and pondweed. Migration begins in late September to early October and concludes when the birds have reached either coast, the Great Lakes, or the Florida panhandle. Hunting methods are the same as for the white-winged.

Black Scoter

Weighing 2¼ to 3¾ pounds (1.01 to 1.69 kg) and measuring 17 to 20 inches (43.2 to 50.8 cm), it is the second largest of the three scoter species. This species is currently in much smaller numbers than its two cousins, but a few are harvested using the same techniques. Diet and migration are the same as for the other two scoter species.

CHAPTER FOUR

Goose Species

During migration, some species of geese have been clocked flying at speeds up to 60 mph (97 kmph) and some may fly at tremendous heights. In flight each flock has a leader of the formation, whether in a V or in long lines across the sky.

Here are four general tips to help identify a goose:

- Goose species are significantly larger than any duck species.

- Their legs are placed even farther forward on the body than those of puddlers, giving geese better balance in traveling on land to graze, as they often do, far from water.

- Geese are wary, and, when feeding, at least one always watches and warns the feeding flock of danger.

- Compared with ducks, necks of geese are longer and bodies are less flattened.

The detailed range maps in this chapter show you exactly where to find each species. You'll see where they breed and spend the summer, and where they winter. A color key for the range maps is shown below.

Key to Goose Range Maps

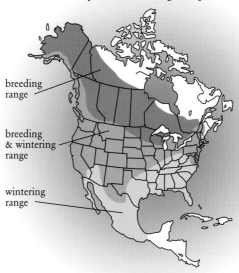

breeding range

breeding & wintering range

wintering range

Canada Goose

With five subspecies, size can vary dramatically. Smaller examples weigh 5 to 7 pounds (2.25 to 3.15 kg) and measure 24 to 28 inches (61 to 71 cm). The larger examples can weigh as much as 10 to 15 pounds (4.5 to 6.75 kg) and measure well over 30 inches (76.2 cm) long. Among the five different subspecies the general appearance for both sexes is the same. Both sport gray bodies, white breasts, white under-tails and black necks, heads and upper-tails. A splash of white along the cheeks completes the markings. The Canada's diet is mostly farm crops such as corn, grass, barley, beans and shoots, with the addition of several species of aquatic vegetation. Migration can seem spotty, as not all Canadas migrate large distances, but rather congregate and feed wherever open water is available. Those more northern birds that do leave the Canadian prairie travel to northern states to winter and as far as Texas and other Gulf Coast states in late October through December. Hunting methods can be divided into two major classifications: field and open-water. Both styles are successful under the correct conditions, as long as decoys and a call are utilized. The Canada is known by most hunters as the easiest bird to call and decoy.

Snow/Blue Goose

Once thought to be two different species, the snow and blue are now considered simply color phases, as these geese feed, weigh, and measure the same, migrate together, and interbreed. On average, the snow/blue weighs 5½ to 7 pounds 2.48 to 3.15 kg) and measures 25 to 27 inches (63.5 to 68.6 cm) long. Both snow sexes display an overall white appearance, with black wingtips and a pink bill and feet. The blue sports an overall grayish blue plumage, with a white head and neck, black wingtips and a pink bill and feet. Neither sex is distinguishable. Their diet is comprised of mostly farm crops as well as seasonal grasses. Migration begins in late September or early October and ends when the birds arrive in the mid-Atlantic states, Gulf Coast states and Mexico in November or early December. Hunting methods are similar to those for the Canada, with the exception of large numbers of decoys being imperative, and (where legal) electronic calling being utilized to draw the enormous migrating flocks. Currently, overpopulation is hindering an overall healthy flock, as northern breeding grounds are being destroyed by overfeeding. Consequently, hunting has been increased in many states and provinces. The discontinuance of employing a plug (three shots or less) is allowed in some provinces.

White-Fronted Goose

Primarily a western species, white-fronteds (often called specklebellies or specks) are rare on the East Coast. Averaging about the same size as a snow or blue, the white-fronted sports a brownish head and body with white-and-black patches or speckles on the breast. As with other goose species, neither sex is distinguishable without capture. Their diet is similar to that of other goose species, with some excess farm crops. Migration begins in late September and into early October, and ends when the birds reach the central valley of California or the coasts of Texas and Louisiana in mid-November or December. Hunting methods are almost identical to those for any other geese, with the high-pitched, almost screaming, call being the only difference.

Brant

Both the American and Black species are saltwater fowl, never venturing too far from the coast. Identification is easy, despite the fact they are the least hunted goose species. Averaging 3 to 4 pounds (1.35 to 1.8 kg), and measuring 18 to 22 inches (45.7 to 55.9 cm) long, they are the second smallest of all the goose species. Both sport blackish brown bodies, with black heads, necks and white collars. Their diets include mostly mollusks, fish and saltwater invertebrates, with the occasional aquatic vegetation. The American brant, which is the eastern species, winters on the Atlantic coast starting mainly in New Jersey south to North Carolina. The Black brant, or western species, winters along the entire Pacific coast. Hunting methods are similar to those used with other goose species, including decoy spreads and calling. The most successful hunter will target backwater salt marshes and bays. Neither species of brant meat is palatable.

CHAPTER FIVE

Decoy Types and Designs

The first decoys were probably made by Canadian Inuits—rough duck imitations out of wood, propped on sticks. Next on the hunting timeline, decoys were assembled using hay or straw, which was formed, colored and tied to best mimic the general shape and essence of the pursued duck or goose. Around this time, the practice of using actual duck or goose skins was becoming a popular means to the necessity of a large spread. Ingenious waterfowlers would regularly save the unused skins of harvested fowl, salt or roughly tan them, and then secure the capes to crude mannequins. Much like the more sophisticated taxidermy practices of today, these mounts were used effectively to entice wary fowl that may have already grown wise to more basic methods.

Slightly later, hunters created better representations of waterfowl through plain carvings of wood and cork, which were painted and used on both land and water. These representations could be carved with or without a keel, adding greater diversity among a spread. While the skin decoys may have looked more realistic, carved "blocks" could be used in both water and on land.

Through trial and error, carvers later created ornate replicas that now grace the mantels and walls of museums and dedicated collectors. While wood was still being heavily utilized during the 1920s, 30s and 40s, pressed cardboard was soon to be developed. By the 1970s, plastics were accepted as the staple decoy material used and continue to be the most common materials employed today. The technological age of the 1990s has added many more opportunities, including wind-powered and battery-powered air and water decoys.

Almost every decoy comes in three major sizes: standard, large and magnum (or standard, magnum and super magnum depending on manufacturer). Their average lengths depending on species are: standard, 15 to 16 inches (38.1 to 40.6 cm); magnum, 18 to 20 inches (45.7 to 50.8 cm); super magnum, 21 inches (53.3 cm) or larger.

The size of decoy to use on a given adventure is based on three criteria:

• time of year

• amount of pressure on the birds

• overall size of the area that is being set

The season usually dictates the correct size a hunter should employ. For early-season hunting the standard size will almost always suffice. Birds usually aren't pressured enough to avoid an average spread. Consequently, the majority of fowl will be coming in much closer to inspect the layout. Also, many hunting seasons that occur during the earlier period are usually for birds that are local, or non-migratory.

Another important variable to consider is the current hunting pressure in the area you plan to hunt. If you are dealing with large public land expanses or fringes of refuges, for example, the birds will have a keen idea of what is routine for a particular area. Once a flock (be it ducks or geese) is shown a certain repeating variable, all can be lost. Here is the perfect opportunity to either increase or decrease the average decoy's size. If experience tells you that the majority of hunters are using magnums or even super magnums to draw birds off a refuge, for example, then the change from big to small can pay huge dividends. On the other hand, if the majority of shooters are using standard-size decoys, the presence of large decoys may be the ticket.

Lastly, be aware of how large or small the area is. Be it a lake, pond, river or field,

each requires a different approach. If the day's location finds you setting decoys along a large lake, perhaps several hundred acres (hectares) or more, the standard size will rarely suffice. Larger magnums or even super magnums will be necessary to attract any passing birds.

Here is a saying to help you remember when to lay a larger decoy: "When lots of blue, small won't do." While silly to remember, it's a simple way to quickly judge a water body and choose an option. Of course, this isn't a hard-and-fast rule. If pressure is heavy and from magnum spreads, then downsizing will be key. Conversely, the decoys needed in a small pothole or pond rarely call for magnum proportions. It does little good to flood a small area with decoys if only a limited number of birds are currently using the area.

While it may sound difficult, using magnum or larger decoys can quickly leave the incoming birds looking for a hole to land. The worst reaction a hunter can receive after completing the work to set a detailed spread is to have the birds land to a far side of the blocks. Once the birds deem the spread inhospitable, getting them to lift and give the decoys another inspection is almost impossible. In these smaller areas, not only will standard-size decoys suffice, but also downsizing the overall number will be necessary.

Simply put, nothing trumps research and scouting when deciding what a particular site will require for success. Each area is filled with differing variables and qualities. Finding and reacting to those variables will separate the hunters eating duck or goose, and the hunters eating crow.

TYPES OF DECOYS

The following section discusses some of the common decoy styles. Every waterfowler should be aware of all the choices available to him or her when heading afield.

FLOATING BLOCK

These are the most common decoy, as they offer the greatest flexibility. This style is made from many different materials, including cork, wood and plastic (the most popular today). Cork is used by hunters creating spreads on larger, choppy waters. This is because cork rides much lower in the water than plastic, and is less apt to tip and sway unnaturally. While the floating-style decoys made of cork afford the hunter these benefits, they can be costly and much less durable than their plastic counterparts. On average, a dozen cork decoys can be as much as three times the average price of a dozen plastics. It can be a difficult choice. For the average hunter, plastic will be the way to go. The true traditionalist may employ a spread of wooden decoys.

Once a particular material type is chosen, you should consider the projected use of the decoy before making the final decision to buy. Most commonly, blocks come in two major forms: keel and keelless.

The keel of a decoy is usually weighted and used to keep the decoy upright. While actual weighted keels are probably the most common, other keel designs include "aqua keel" styles, whereby holes are drilled into the keel to allow water to penetrate it. The decoy is stabilized by the surrounding water. Many hunters who pack in their decoys, or walk longer distances to hunt prefer these lighter models.

A keelless decoy can seem impossible to use at first, but with practice it can be a real asset. Being able to utilize the spread in water and on land is a huge asset when hunting late-season, pressured birds. Decoys can simply sit on land, rocks, ice or mud, while also being set in water. Obviously, the only downfall is when hunting choppy or rough water. These decoys have been known to roll or pitch unnaturally when confronted with these conditions.

A variation, the suction-keel style has the ability to function with the same versatility as the keelless, but instead of uncontrolled floating, the underside of the decoy has a carved channel. Through this design, air is trapped within this channel, creating a vacuum. Through suction, the decoy rides naturally upon the water's surface. This decoy isn't suited for extremely rough water.

Styles and Depictions

The most obvious benefit to using blocks is their many different poses, including all species of pursued waterfowl as well as several different confidence species. Many keelless decoys not only stand or sit on land, but on water as well. Sleeping, feeding and even flying fowl are now represented by this decoy design.

SHELL

Less common to the majority of duck hunters, shell-style decoys have taken the goose hunting world by storm. This is not to imply that "shells" don't have a place in the duck blind as well. Many shell-style duck decoys are made for the field hunter pursuing mallards and blacks. However, due to the shell's portability and light weight, many goose hunters that demand larger field spreads and prefer less work, have hugely popularized this design.

Material selection is simple, as the majority of shells are made of plastic, and only a minute number of brands are made of pressed cardboard. Much like the keelless block-style design, shells have a hard body. The molds are quite similar in appearance, yet with one major difference: shells are completely hollow. Much like a four-sided building with no floor, they merely sit on their frames.

Unlike their floating counterparts, shells are designed to be placed on land or on slightly flooded ground. They are not used very often when hunting larger water or in many types of float hunting. In the southern United States, "staked" shells (decoys that employ a plastic or wooden stake for stability) are regularly placed in flooded rice or bean fields where water levels don't exceed 12 to 18 inches (30.5 to 45.7 cm). The ability to stake shells slightly above water level in these flooded areas is a key element for success.

Because of their portable nature, shells also work well as complements to existing spreads. Shells are a great choice when trying to achieve the look of a larger flock or filling open spots along river banks, sand dunes or mud flats. Before the photo-silhouette decoy craze, shells were the majority of a field gunner's gear. Having the ability to position a few hundred decoys in less than an hour was and still is a huge asset. The added benefit that shells easily stack on top of one another for storage also makes them popular.

Styles and Depictions

While shell-style decoys do have the benefit of being light in weight and easy to store during the off-season, actual depictions are limited. On average, shells are offered in five major positions: sentry, feeding, resting, sleeping and calling. While it may seem that there are very few differences between the block and the shell in the way of poses, it should be remembered that the shell style can't be modified to depict anything other than the whole bird. The absence of bobbling duck rumps (half-body feeder blocks), jerk cords or outstretched wings, puts these decoys at a slight disadvantage. Nonetheless, even with today's decoy innovations, shells will always have a use, if for nothing else than as spread fillers.

Success is more than matching a particular decoy with the intended target bird. Through years of research, both biologists and hunters have found strict correlations between overall flock comfort and the acceptance of other species in their midst. "Birds of a feather" is not always true. For the majority of species, the old maxim of "puddle ducks with puddle ducks and divers with divers" is still correct, though each category encompasses many different species. And for the hunter, the ability to introduce a surprise is invaluable when the birds aren't cooperating. For many, the bird they are targeting is the only bird that they have decoys for. This is a huge mistake!

Besides the obvious fact that having multiple species in an arsenal affords the hunter multi-species hunting, it also increases confidence. This is the variable a hunter is conquering when setting multiple species in one hole. The intention may be to only harvest green-head mallards, for example, but through the use of such simulated allies as gadwalls, black ducks and teal, the hunter is creating the illusion of a happy pothole or waterway. It's these common puddle species that a mallard will regularly land and feed with. It's the calling and body language of these other species that the mallard will study before landing.

Another more dramatic example, usually very beneficial to the hunter, is mixing goose decoys among a duck spread. While ducks prefer to land and mingle among other equally sized ducks, the

presence of the goose flock is proof that there is no danger close by. The opposite approach, using duck decoys among a goose spread is also very effective.

Unfortunately, this strategy can work against the hunter as well. Some species prefer segregated flocking, or dislike a particular species. A great example of this is seen with the wood duck. While mallards feel more than comfortable landing and feeding among wood ducks and other puddle species, wood ducks themselves prefer to be in smaller segregated pairs or flocks.

This also holds true for all species of geese. While differing goose species can be seen feeding among each other in the same field, each species is usually flocked within their species. It's not very often that flocks of snows and Canadas are wing-to-wing, happily feeding. Noted waterfowl expert and call fabricator, Rod Haydel, once brought this same scenario to my attention regarding the compatibility of white-fronted geese and snows. Known as the least accepting of other species, snows regularly fight with nearby white-fronteds. Consequently, white-fronteds that choose to feed in the same areas usually land and feed in smaller groups to one side of the snow flock—not helpful to the hunter.

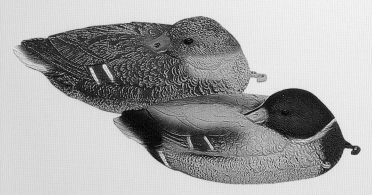

FULL BODY

Heavy, bulky, hard-to-store and expensive, the full body design has many drawbacks. But they have one huge benefit: they are some of the most realistic decoys on the market today. Designed with anatomical perfection, full bodies appear in all styles as the entire bird. For the hunter willing to tote this larger and heavier design, this is sure to outweigh the physical hardship. Before you make the decision to buy, there are a few more issues to examine:

First, and foremost, can you afford this style? On average, it is sold in lots of four for $100.00 or more. Unless you believe you can be successful with a mere handful, you might want to consider another option.

Second, full-bodied decoys are difficult to store. Not designed to fully collapse or stack, they must be hung in decoy sacks to keep them secure. While some recent models have the option of dismantling the head and neck from the decoy, you are still left with the chore of finding a home for body and legs.

Third, can you heft them into and out of the field? Statistics show that the average age of today's hunter is far into his or her fifties–or older. Many hunters have traded in back strength for all-terrain-vehicles or non-motorized garden carts to transport their spreads.

Fortunately, there is one huge advantage to owning full-bodied decoys, especially for the multi-season hunter: versatility. The common design that utilizes large feet or pedestals that support the decoy on ice or frozen ground is a component

that only this style can claim. No need to struggle with bending stakes or pre-drilling holes before setting one on the ice or rock-hard ground. Just lay out the decoys and settle back for the action.

One way to attract more birds is to employ more full-bodied decoys, and fewer of the more common designs. Waterfowl can become familiar with and aware of major differences among a hunter's spread. If birds see silhouettes or shells used on a regular basis, the process of switching your spread to full body imposters can be hugely successful. Of course, the opposite can also hold true and full-bodied decoys can be over-used.

Styles and Depictions

Much like the floating-block style, full-bodied decoys have many different positions. Low century, high century, active, semi-active, feeding and stretch-neck feeders are just some of the positions available. Having the benefit of multiple depictions is an asset when targeting educated, or late-season birds. Most hunters appreciate the lifelike and detailed feather pattern this style displays.

SILHOUETTE

One of the first styles to be employed by a hunter, silhouettes have since proved to be one of the most preferred designs utilized today. Early models were homemade wooden renditions that were traced and cut from a piece of plywood, painted, and then staked with the scrap. Today's now-standard plastic, photo-imaged models have even hunters looking twice.

Used by waterfowlers pursuing species that require large decoy spreads, the silhouette offers increased packing ease. Because silhouettes are lighter than shells or blocks, easier to transport, easier to store and even more realistic, the majority of hunters who once relied on the shell's convenience and productivity have since converted their spreads to silhouettes.

Granted, silhouettes will never completely replace any decoy—while they do boast the most realistic detail available, they still remain only two dimensional. Fowl flying directly overhead may at first glance not even see the "birds" below. To combat this common problem, the experienced waterfowler sets many silhouettes in numerous positions and differing angles, to both cover as much ground as possible and avoid any chance of unseen decoys. The other technique of

slightly tilting the decoy at a 45-degree angle allows more surface area to be viewed by passing fowl. One caveat: the decoy should not be laid on its side or tilted farther than the standard 45 degrees. You don't want to give the impression of wounded or dead fowl, but rather a more viewable surface area.

Styles and Depictions

To cope with the difficulty of manufacturing all silhouettes in two-dimensional form, many companies have created only a couple poses. The most obvious and easiest to create is the sentry. The other is the feeding pose.

Used in the same manner as multi-species decoying, the use of non-hunted species decoys such as great blue herons, swans, cranes, crows and seagulls can provide a huge advantage. These decoys drive heavily pressured birds into spreads that they may not otherwise commit to. Of course, not all confidence species work everywhere. It's important to match the species of decoy to the area. Many hunters make the mistake of combining a confidence decoy that doesn't match the most common species of bird.

A good example of this was seen several years ago as decoy manufacturers began to design and sell various confidence decoy models. Some hunters became caught up in the craze and wanted to experiment with different species and models. Needless to say, too many hunters purchased species of decoys that weren't common, or even native, to their target area. Consequently, instead of fowl flocking to the "secure" area, birds avoided those spreads entirely.

It isn't difficult to locate and match the appropriate species. One or two pre-hunt trips to the marsh will be enough to make a decision. While there, observe the area, and the most common bird species. Are there great blue herons standing in the shallows? Are cranes feeding in the nearby fields? Do flocks of seagulls fill the bays and setbacks? It's simple observations like these that will save both money and fowl in the following seasons. Once a species is located, all that is left is purchasing the corresponding decoy before the season starts.

MECHANICAL

This style incorporates more and dramatically differ-ent designs than any other category of decoy. Some examples are spinning winged, swimming and quiv-ering. Despite their overall popularity, this style has sparked various debates. Some states have outlawed motorized decoys, calling them an unsportsmanlike method of lure. Whether or not you favor these decoys, knowledge of them is a must in order to better understand the perfect spread.

Mechanical decoys all have one obvious attribute in common: being mechanical. Fueled by a battery source or wind, they propel one of the decoy's body parts to imitate a living bird. Whether via wings that spin, a body that swims, or some other related method, mechanicals are designed to move freely on their own. Mojo Decoys and RoboDuk were two of the first companies to create and dis-tribute a mechanical decoy. Initially, all models were the standard spinning-wing designs. Today, hunters are able to utilize both standard and water models. Mechanical water decoys can be a huge boost when targeting wary birds. While the use of jerk cords has been employed for years, the use of mechanical water decoys is relatively new, and birds don't tend to shy from them.

It was until just recently that only one decoy could work off a single battery source. Now, thanks to accessories such as Cabela's Mallard Machine and Spinning Wing System, multiple decoys can depict a more lifelike appearance. Both units are designed to hold two to three decoys and be used in different applications. The Mallard Machine is a prop-driven water unit that shakes, dives and quivers decoys to give them a lifelike appearance. The Spinning Wing System is a spinning airborne unit that spins two spinning-wing decoys in a 10-foot (3-m) circle. While nei-ther of these units exactly fits the definition of a mechanical decoy, their designs and characteris-tics give the hunter many more mechanical choic-es and spread depictions when targeting wary birds.

Because these decoys are more complicated and using multiple decoys is best, a sizeable investment used to be required to properly outfit a common spread. Fortunately, they have dropped in price, and it's now affordable for the most modest gunner to employ the recommended two or three units.

Styles and Depictions

Mechanicals can be powered in three ways: by battery, wind or hand. Like the bird species they regularly attract, there are more designs and mod-els than any other decoy type on the market today. At first glance this type may seem void of many depictions, since no manufacturer has produced any free-walking or multi-pose mechanical decoys. But you'll find that the benefits of motion alone will give you a big advantage in the field.

The most simple of all mechanical models is the quiver magnet. Shaped like a hockey puck, the internal electric motor is coupled with eccentric weights that shake and quiver when the unit is activated. This product comes in two models. The first is designed to be slipped into the back of a floating-block-style decoy: simply cut a small slit, turn it on, and slide the magnet into the decoy. Once placed in the water, the decoy will shimmy and shake like a feeding bird. The other model is a floating unit that works on the same principle, but doesn't require inserting into another decoy. Sev-eral of these can be placed throughout a spread to insinuate several feeding birds.

Similar in effect, TurboJet Duck Decoys produces a block-style decoy that mimics the feeding pattern of a duck. Employing battery-operated jet propulsion, the decoy swims back and forth and discharges bubbles like a feeding duck. Using the anchor line as a guide, the decoy swims until reaching the end of the anchor cord, and then returns to its original position. TurboJet doesn't yet manufacture a goose counterpart, but the mallard drake and hen models are very effective.

Spinning Wing decoys were the original mechanical options on the market. Today this brand accounts for ninety percent of all spinning-wing decoys using the depiction of a landing mallard duck, with wings that spin as if the bird were landing. Companies such as RoboDuk and Mojo Decoys offer spinning-wing goose decoys, as well as other duck species. Mojo's green-winged teal is a great supplement when hunting multiple puddle duck species.

Initially, spinning-wing decoys were activated by a switch on the breast or under-side of the decoy. Today, these decoys have remote control from a few hundred feet (meters) away. While most spinning-wing designs are anchored by a single stake, which can limit their use to land or shallow water, Mojo has designed a floating rendition of the spinning wing–Mojo Floater. Solving all the issues associated with employing a spinning-wing decoy in deep water, the Mojo Floater uses the same spinning-wing technology, but rather with a floating-block-style decoy attached to a camouflage bladder. Anchored in the same fashion as a common floating decoy, the Mojo Floater can be set and utilized among other floating blocks. One note: Be sure to check the hunting laws for the state or province you plan to hunt, as some have outlawed this style of decoy.

Mechanicals combining the concepts of both battery power and wind power have come into vogue. Lucky Duck has designed a wind-powered decoy similar to a battery-powered spinning-wind decoy, but uses wind instead. The Air Lucky is a pole-stabilized spinning-wing decoy that utilizes a two-blade Turbo Wing design. Upon the slightest breeze, the wings come to life.

Beginning with the popular jerk-cord concept, manual mechanics are still used today. The flapping-wing Canada goose decoy made by Wing Wavers is a set of wings and tail that attach to a silhouette body (included). Activated by a jerk cord, the wings wave up and down, like a stretching or landing goose. This decoy is a great complement to any early-season Canada spread. Wing Wavers exclusively makes Canada goose models. Higdon Finisher Flaps also makes a flapping-wing model, operated by hand to spin the wings. Wing Keepers ensure the upper darker sections of wings continually spin back naturally upon the completion of the revolution. These wings are guaranteed to stay synchronized and natural.

RAG

Decoys can't be any simpler than these. They are used almost entirely by goose hunters for creating enormous spreads of 1,000 or more when hunting large areas. Created by the Texas Rag Decoy Company, the Texas Rag is, in essence, a large windsock made of a one-piece waterproof, non-sheen material. Stakes are also offered by the manufacturer, sold separately. Not only are these decoys the lightest on the market, they are also the least expensive. When creating snow spreads of several hundred decoys or more, this cost is a fraction of any other design on the market today.

While the general design may seem elementary, the resulting look and motion is quite sophisticated. Rags are staked with the front of the decoy (open end) set into the wind. With a breeze, the decoy slightly lifts from the ground and sways from side to side like a feeding goose. A head-on view of the decoys may not be impressive to the human eye but, from behind, they appear to be a flock of feeding geese.

All that is required to set an entire flock of several hundred are the corresponding stakes. In a pinch, utilizing surrounding cornstalks or tall wheat stubble can work as substitute stakes. Simply clear a 2-foot (61-cm) circle around each decoy, leaving a single stalk or small bunch of wheat or other stiff grass as the needed support. While this may not suffice on a windy day, it has been known to save the outing for a forgetful hunter.

Styles and Depictions

Because of its design simplicity, there is only one possible pose but the stake can be set shallower in the soil to insinuate the goose to be standing, or sunken deeper to mimic resting, sleeping or feeding birds. Most importantly, rags are offered in every color combination necessary to mimic any goose species.

KITE

These decoys are tethered, and glide off wind currents. Picture a basic decoy spread. Set in the basic fishhook or half-moon pattern, some spinning-wing decoys to the sides and a confidence decoy set on the outer fringe. But what's in the sky to imitate natural moving or landing birds? In a large flock, birds are regularly lifting and relocating to other sections. They leave members of their species or others that are violent, or possibly to relocate to an area with more food. Birds never simply stay put or walk when situated in larger migratory groups. Don't forget to fill at least a small section of air space over a large spread. It's been my experience that using a kite for almost any spread size will pay huge benefits when trying to grab the attention of distant or extremely high birds. When hunting prairie regions, I have found kites to be a requirement. Large amounts of movement with decoys 20 feet (6 m) or higher up in the sky will make visibility of the overall spread that much clearer.

Styles and Depictions

Given the simple nature of this object, there are no differing depictions and very few designs. Similar to a child's kite, these decoys are designed with an internal frame and form-fitting plastic or weatherproof material. Jackite manufactures kites in both a Canada goose and mallard pattern. Outlaw Decoys has also devised a model of kite that has proven to be very effective. It is offered in the Canada, mallard and snow goose pattern.

FLAG

Flagging is one of the best methods for finishing your waterfowl decoying. A simple design, the flag is usually composed of some form of appropriately colored cotton or nylon material, a cross-bar and a handle. For Canada geese, use flat black or black with a white stripe on the lower tail section. For snow geese, use a full piece of white material or a piece of white material with black wing sections. While you can purchase a manufactured flag, creating your own couldn't be easier—just two dowels and a piece of material.

Many hunters don't use flags, but this method of decoying has proven to be a necessity when hunting both Canada snows and specklebellies. These big geese react well to large amounts of movement around a decoy spread. This is not to suggest that ducks won't adhere to the same theory. Many duck species—including mallards, blacks and gadwalls—will investigate and later commit to a flagged spread. Flagging can be done almost until the last lay-down calls are made to any goose species, but I have found that ducks are slightly less forgiving of the movement, and hunters should stop flagging once the ducks have committed to their spread.

While kites tend to be more successful when employed over a large spread, flagging has proven to be useful over as few as two decoys. When hunting specklebellies, using two to four decoys is all that is usually necessary. Couple that modest spread with one of two hunters flagging and a spread literally comes to life. Much like kiting, flagging is another method to ensure passing birds will see and hopefully investigate a properly set decoy spread.

Styles and Depictions

Much like the kite, this decoy is really too simple to offer a multitude of designs or models. All models, regardless of manufacturer, have a flag, cross-bar and handle. In addition, many models have been upgraded to include better detail, better shaping, and fiberglass cross-bars to ensure a more lifelike presentation.

Outlaw Decoys manufacturers the T-Flag, which is one of the most realistic flags available today. Offered in a couple different species, the T-Flag is another tool to entice decoy-shy fowl. Hunter's View Goose Flag is made of Rip-Stop nylon secured with plastic cross-bars. Hunter's View is not only dependable, but an extremely affordable choice when outfitting a large spread.

CHAPTER SIX

Decoy Spreads and Strategies

For seasoned waterfowlers and novices alike, this facet of our sport is one of the most popular. It's been said that too much emphasis is put on calling and too little on proper decoy selection and placement. While calling is one of the most integral pieces of a successfully completed waterfowling puzzle, it's the decoy spread and selection that is the framework or foundation necessary for continued success. One can call with the skill and charisma of a concert performer and never take a duck or goose. It's the behind-the-scenes preparatory work and knowledge that will ensure victory in the end. Now, I'm not referring to scouting or even proper blind placement. While these are also necessities for a successful outing, these topics will be covered in later sections. Here are a few general tips:

First and most important, decoys should always be faced into the wind. This holds true for all spread scenarios. Birds need to land and take off into the wind. Consequently, birds will feed, rest and socialize faced into the existing wind currents. Moving decoys that are no longer facing into the wind will be necessary to pull off a realistic layout. Also, a hunter won't continue to be successful with only the knowledge of hunting one spread type of scenario.

Second, decoy spacing fluctuates from one season's period to another, as both ducks and geese adapt to changing conditions. While many hunters see spacing as simply what the birds are doing on a particular day, the science behind it lies in ambient temperature. For instance, how often have birds seemed sparsely spaced during warmer, or mild conditions? How often have birds been huddled tightly together during periods of stormy or cooler weather? It's temperature that mainly dictates how birds will be situated on a particular field or water body. During warmer temperatures the need to conserve body heat isn't a concern, and birds move freely. During periods of cooler weather, birds flock tightly to conserve energy. This same behavior can be seen when heavy hunting pressure is present. Understanding this variable may help change a day of few birds into a day to remember.

There are four major decoy patterns for puddle ducks and diving ducks–fishhook, half-moon, half-circle and strung-out patterns. These four will be used in all of the duck hunting scenarios described later.

For geese, those same four can be employed, plus two for specifically targeting geese–family grouping and rafting (seen occasionally for ducks but mostly used with goose hunting and confidence sets).

Here is a brief description of each pattern:

- **Fishhook.** This pattern is comprised of decoys beginning in the form of a long line and swinging into a hooked shape, either right or left.

- **Half Moon.** This pattern is comprised of decoys that are set in the shape of a half moon. Usually the blind is positioned in the middle of the decoys, though this can fluctuate with surrounding cover.

- **Half Circle.** Similar to half-moon patterning, but with a more circular design.

- **Strung Out.** This is used almost exclusively by diver ducks. It is comprised of several dozen decoys placed on a long line and set in place to represent natural diver postures.

- **Family Group.** Used exclusively by goose hunters, it mimics geese flocked and feeding in small family groups. Here, decoys are placed in alternating positions (still into the wind) in small, tight clusters.

- **Rafting.** It's most often used to represent geese that are resting or feeding later in the season. Also seen during later months when ducks are escaping tight hunting pressure in the middle of a large lake or pond. These decoys should be attached with the same long lines as in strung-out patterning, but with birds much tighter to each other. Very little water should be seen between each bird. While this pattern can be hunted over during the later periods of the season, especially when hunting from a boat, it's used mainly to create "confidence rafts," which are small groups of confidence species such as Canada geese or gadwalls within a mallard spread.

PUDDLERS

As a rule, puddle ducks prefer smaller water than diving ducks; even the shallowest slough or tiniest creek may offer top-rate hunting. But puddlers are also found on some of North America's largest waters, including the Great Lakes and Utah's Great Salt Lake. While divers are comfortable riding out big waves in open water, puddlers are usually found in calm water. In windy weather, they seek shelter along a lee shore.

In setting decoys for puddle ducks, remember that puddlers rest in looser groups than divers, so your decoys can be spread out much more. Some hunters leave as much as 10 feet (3 m) between individual blocks.

POTHOLE AND SMALL WATER SETS

Aside from fooling Canada geese, hunting puddlers in a hand-to-hand situation is one of my favorite ways to hunt ducks. It's the close proximity of the hunter to the duck that regularly draws me to hunt smaller and lesser-known locations. Besides having access to shots that are usually under 30 yards (27.3 m), smaller locations are usually under-hunted, and require far fewer decoys than the more standard lake, pond or feed field scenarios.

For ease of example, let's assume that this location is in the Northeast. This pothole could be a small flooded beaver swamp, lesser-known wetland or very small pond. The water flow is slow to standing, and heavy vegetation lines the outline of the bank. Having scouted the day before, the hunter locates a small weedy point that breaks the shore's continuous edge, creating a small bay. Besides knowing the topography, the hunter also observes ducks using this area as a feeding and roosting zone just before the end of shooting light.

This is a great example of needing only a small number of decoys to almost guarantee success. When first setting the spread, the hunter should worry little about any blind, as the cattails on the point will be an excellent form of cover. The hunter can stand or hunch down until finding the shot. Using only 12 to 18 mallard decoys or a mixture of puddler decoys will be all that's needed.

Placement should be simple, as most of these locations are relatively shallow. Position the ducks in a half-moon or half-circle pattern (depending on topography). Starting in the bay and then working back toward the point and blind, the last few decoys should clear the point and continue the pattern slightly past it. The confidence decoys can range from a couple representatives, to a small army, depending on what the particular area and present hunting pressure dictate.

On average, for a mid-season or even late-season hunt, throwing a half dozen Canada geese floaters to the far right or left of the duck decoys will be a great addition. Another alternative is to place a great blue heron on the outer edge of the spread. This is known as the ultimate confidence decoy, and while it should never be placed directly in the middle of the spread (ducks won't land at their feet) placing one on the side is effective. Another option, where legal, is the addition of a mechanical decoy directly in the middle of the spread. This is probably the best thing a hunter can do to ensure success in these smaller areas.

While it may seem overdone to use a mechanical in such a small area, I'm reminded of an old poker proverb: "Why beat them with kings if you can beat them with aces?" There is nothing wrong with adding a wild card in any situation. Adding motion on the edge of the landing pocket is effective at both roosting and early-morning feed sites.

While hunters should prefer the wind at their back or flowing from their right or left, this can't always be controlled; especially in these smaller swamp or pothole situations. As long as the hunter locates some form of topography to utilize, and remembers to leave a landing pocket, this set will work on a regular basis.

POND AND LAKE SETS

If there was ever a scenario that required the assistance of many other sets to be routinely successful, it would be this one. Hunting puddle ducks on larger water bodies requires knowledge and strategy far beyond any other scenario. I have often been asked why I feel these locations demand more from the hunter, and always my answer is simple: Change! Because of their size, both lakes and ponds can act as roosting habitat, feed zones, resting areas for local birds and migrants. Depending on the time of season and level of hunting pressure, a prepared hunter should use both a variety of species as well as varying decoy numbers.

To best illustrate this, let's assume that the water body is a large lake near the Canadian–U.S. border, known for both migrants as well as a steady local population. It's mid-October and very little pressure has been placed on the majority of the lake. After doing the necessary preliminary scouting, a medium-size bay is located approximately 300 yards (273 m) from a cattail-laden setback. Knowing there are both feeding and roosting ducks that travel to and from that area, this bay seems like a viable choice. The spread will attract both traveling ducks trying to reach the setback as well as any ducks traveling the main lake.

When confronted with the task of decoying a large area, especially when there is more than one possible travel route, it's important that the spread have more than one option for the ducks to land. In this situation, a fishhook (or "J") pattern will be the best bet. The fishhook pattern is necessary for drawing birds from longer distances, as it can cover a larger surface area with fewer decoys. A double fishhook can be used for even better results. "Double" fishhook refers to simply adding another bend on the other side of the line, turning the pattern into more of an anchor shape. This technique is more apt to lure birds from both sides of the water body, as well as supply more areas for them to land.

Decoy numbers will be drastically different. Utilizing two to three dozen decoys, at minimum, will be necessary in order to replicate a natural big-water flock. While mallards will probably be the dominant species choice, adding teal, black duck and a smattering of wood duck decoys will best represent the common puddle species of a particular area.

Position the blind or boat (remember, the area is much deeper than a pothole) at the end of the shank, where the hookeye sits. Imagine the birds to be attached to a giant fish line. In this position, with proper calling, the hunter is able to "reel" the birds right down the line. The decoy spread shouldn't be any longer than 30 to 40 yards (27.3 to 36.4 m). This medium distance will reduce the chance of crippling birds, which is more common at longer yardages.

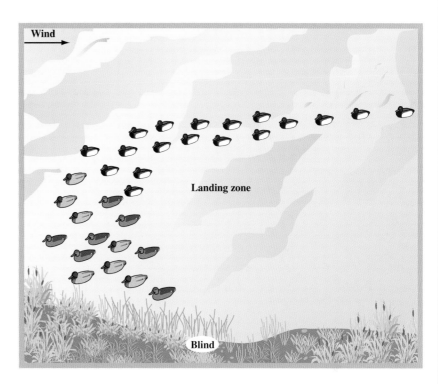

Adding some form of a mechanical decoy will not only attract more birds, but may reduce the number of cripples. Use at least one, and preferably two or three, mechanicals, and position them on either side and in the middle of the spread. Hunting large areas requires head-turning realism and appeal. There is no better way to achieve this than with some form of movement. Conversely, remember that too much movement can hurt as much as help. While a duck's brain is approximately the size of an almond, it can easily tell if a spread has more movement that a natural flock. You should use no more than four mechanicals when hunting very large spreads. When employing so many decoys, use the new remote control models, which can be activated and deactivated upon the presence of birds. It's this stop-and-go movement that has proven to be the most seductive.

Once the blind and main decoy spread is complete, adding a confidence decoy or spread can be your ace in the hole. Creating a mini spread of floating Canadas or snow geese floater decoys on one edge of the spread can up your odds. Depending on average depth, placing a great blue heron decoy back away from the spread(s) is also a good idea. By the way, the use of coots as confidence decoys works very well. Coots prefer larger water to feed and rest in, so placing a pair of coots to the opposite side of the geese will add even more realism.

The decoy size you choose will vary depending on hunting pressure and water size. Remember the good rule of size versus time of year. Whether the lake or large pond is hunted hard or not, if the hunt is during the later season and migrants are present, employing larger decoys will be necessary to grab their attention and funnel them into the spread. Otherwise, a large spread of standard-size decoys will suffice.

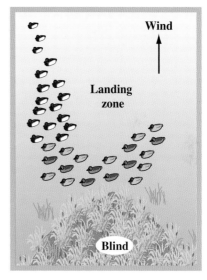

You can set a J-hook along a straight shoreline, as long as the wind is blowing parallel to shore (top). The leg of the J should be aligned with the wind, and the pocket of the J, where the birds will usually land, should be directly in front of the blind. With the wind blowing offshore from a point (bottom), set a group of decoys just off the tip. Then, run a line of decoys straight out into the lake, forming a short J-hook. Gradually increase the spacing between the blocks as you go out. This spread is similar to the J-hook used for big-water divers, but it is shorter and contains fewer blocks.

When setting decoys for puddle ducks along the edge or in setbacks of an average-size river, spread choice and overall presentation may be limited. Due to the river's main current, the hunter trying to create the realism seen in most river feeding and resting zones will be forced to adhere to many diver duck hunting principles. Most obvious is the need to securely anchor several sets of decoys. This is more difficult when compared to the slack water of most puddle sets. But with a few simple techniques, river hunting can be just as easy.

For this scenario, let's assume that the hunter has located a medium- to large-size creek. It's located in the southern United States, where crop fields commonly lie adjacent to the main flow, attracting a plethora of waterfowl species. Farther on, a small setback and sandy point seem to hold resting birds, as large amounts of tracks and droppings prove. Not just in the South, but also in the East and Midwest, this scenario holds birds throughout the entire season. Because rivers are the last to freeze (where cold enough), birds regularly flock to these areas to not only water and feed, but also to escape the hunting pressure found in nearby fields or larger water bodies.

In our example, decoy numbers and selection may seem overzealous, but a fair number will be necessary to draw passing birds. Three or four dozen decoys isn't uncommon, with two to three dozen representing puddle species only. In these river locations many different species congregate. Consequently, you need a minimum of three different decoy species.

Most commonly mallards, blacks, wood ducks and the less-desirable fish-eating species (common and hooded mergansers) utilize this habitat. On larger rivers not only will these birds be present, but also teal and geese. Positioning and proper anchoring techniques differ from one river to the next, but overall one premise remains: decoys need to be secure! Not securing the decoys correctly will eventually cause the entire spread to drift to one side or, worse, send them down the river. Therefore, diver decoy rigging is necessary for not only set aesthetics, but for insurance.

Unlike the common slack-water puddle set, ducks will spend little time examining a decoy set before continuing down the creek. Using the river bottom as the main flyway, ducks will be cruising from one crop field to the next, merely eyeing what's below. This is where medium to long lines of decoys should be placed and anchored on the edge of the current.

Creating a main line, attach 8 to 12 decoys in 2- to 3-foot (60 to 91 cm) intervals. Don't be afraid to mix it up and position a few closer and possibly a couple farther apart. The more realistic, the better. With this line, only one large anchor is necessary to secure the flock, as the decoys will drift back and face into the current. A 1- to 2-pound (0.45 to 0.9 kg) anchor will suffice. With this set of decoys, you are trying to imitate a flock of birds that may have just landed or swam in to join the others.

Next, moving several feet (meters) back from the current, position single puddle blocks on the edge of the setback or slack water. This is where the landing hole should be located. The shooter needs to make sure either a blind or natural cover is present nearby. These blocks should mimic resting or feeding birds. Approximately 18 to 24 decoys should be placed in the setback. Depending on the topography, and where the surrounding crop fields lie in position to the river, a half-moon set will usually work best, with the opening facing the main channel.

Also, utilizing the sand point will be key in constructing a realistic spread. It's on dry land that not only some form of mechanical decoy should be placed (unless the water is shallow enough to place it within the pattern), but also a set of confidence decoys to complete the scheme. Depending on geography, Canada geese decoys are usually best suited for this scenario. Using rivers and nearby crop fields themselves, they are regularly seen

in these areas. Keeping this in mind, placing 6 to 12 full body Canada decoys on the point or other dry place nicely represents a safe area.

Another option if the point or dry ground is within shooting range, is to place a dozen or more mallard silhouette decoys in the position of the geese. Placing them in no particular pattern, but rather as if they are just roving and feeding, will add even more realism and depth to the spread.

FEED FIELD SETS

Creating a spread in a feed field is dramatically different from any water presentations. First, decoy choice is usually very limited. No quiver magnets or jerk cords work, and unless the ground is soft, keeled decoys will lean and look unnatural. For this example, let's assume that it's late October where large tracts of corn and wheat fields are at the height of harvest, and large flocks of puddle ducks have found the excess crops and are regularly feeding. From past experience, the hunter knows the feeding schedule for a particular cornfield is from early morning to just before dark, with a lull during midday. While experience says to pack it in during the slower periods of late morning and early afternoon, the possibility for migrants or a

bonus goose flock is too great to leave. It's in your best interest to stay in place all day.

Decoy selection in this case is easy, as most won't suffice for this application. Most commonly, mallard or black duck shells make up the majority of a field spread. Next, silhouettes can be used, along with suction-bottom keeless decoys. Having the availability of more than one style will give the set more dimension and a natural appearance.

When setting in a field scenario, the average shooter may not know or understand why a particular set is more productive than another. Patterning, like any other facet of strategic waterfowling, is dictated by the results found while scouting.

Using field or water decoys, make a spread with one or two 10- to 15-yard- wide (9 to 14 m) openings on the downwind side. Wearing camo clothing, lie among the decoys or use a pit blind for cover. The ducks will approach from the downwind side and try to land in the openings.

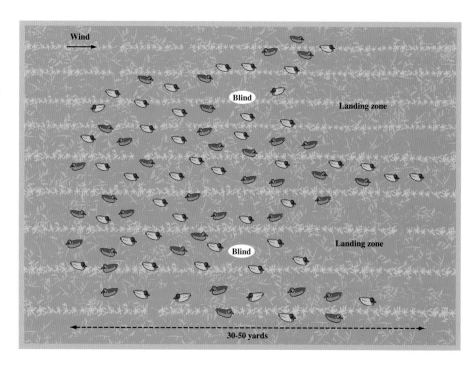

When hunting a dry food source such as a crop field, the availability of water should be first and foremost in the hunter's mind. Without water, the birds wouldn't be able to feed and survive in the area. Consequently, the proper decoy pattern will be clearly dictated by those other variables.

Confidence decoys can seem out of place here, as the majority are designed for water applications. Faced with this dilemma, I spent several seasons experimenting with several different styles and species types. First trying waterfowl species, I found them to work only on occasion. Ducks weren't totally accepting of the species they mostly acquainted with water. After several trials, I found the answer: turkeys and crows. Yes, seriously! These two birds set 25 yards (22.75 m) or farther away from the main spread are an excellent method for attracting decoy-shy birds. Setting a small flock of crows, or a couple turkey decoys to the far side, indicates a safe and secure atmosphere. Finding a few trees not far from the spread and adding crow decoys to the limbs can create even more realism.

Assuming there is a water source at the eastern end of the field, the opening (or landing pocket) should be facing the area from which they will be

traveling (east). Once you learn the geography, it makes little difference what pattern is used, as long as you avoid the strung-out and fishhook patterns. These two are used almost exclusively for water sets and have little application to any land scenarios. Half-moons and half-circles work well, as the opening can be faced toward the water flyways. If multiple water sources are present, a double-horseshoe set will intercept both flight patterns.

Your blind should not be far from the landing pocket(s). Sitting in the center of the spread, not far from the opening, will guarantee optimum shooting opportunities, as well as best conceal your position. Remember, you need to be concealed well. Placing several magnum-size decoys nearby not only breaks up your silhouette but also suggests the presence of a small hump or high spot in the field. One of the best methods I have found to camouflage hunters when field hunting is by using the Avery Finisher Blind. Not only are they comfortable, but they can be camouflaged to blend in with almost any background. I have even rubbed mud on the outside to better mimic the muddy field I was lying in. The canvas strapping on the outside also accepts grasses or cornstalks to create an even better disguise.

In my opinion, there is no other scenario where the conditions can help or horribly hinder a waterfowler more than when hunting flooded timber. But with detailed pre-hunt conditions scouting you will dramatically increase your odds of success—whatever the species you're after.

Expert waterfowler and call manufacturer, Will Primos, once gave me the southern perspective on hunting flooded timber. The first thing he told me was that when decoying puddle ducks, water depth is very important. Will continued by explaining the necessity for water depths of 2 to 2½ feet (0.6- to 0.75 m). Needing to be able to reach the bottom, the majority of puddlers won't comfortably land where they have to work for food.

Constructing a convincing decoy set is the next challenge. It's been discovered that very few decoys are necessary to pull ducks out of the sky and into a flooded hole. Using single rigging and a dozen decoys or fewer, any hunter can create realism with very little equipment. Even as few as three or four may draw birds into extremely tight quarters. As with any set, add more for a larger hole.

Patterning is slightly different when mimicking timber ducks. While the need to establish a distinguishable pattern and landing pocket was necessary for the more open scenarios, decoying ducks in timber requires far less preparation.

Timber protocol requires the decoys be strewn about, as if the ducks were dabbling. Don't forget to leave a space for oncoming ducks to land, so the decoys pattern doesn't seem haphazard, looking as if a pocket was forgotten. Along this pocket, a standing tree or blow-down will suffice for a blind. Many hunters simply stand directly against a tree trunk, blending in until the shot.

For flooded timber hunting, mechanicals are necessary, especially if hunting within close proximity of competition. Descent calling and the few decoys strewn about won't always be enough to pull flocks. Quite often, it's the added movement that ultimately brings success. Most commonly, spinning-wing or paddling decoys work excellently for this scenario. Also common are quiver magnets, which work well when simulating a feeding flock. Merely tossing a few around the interior and exterior of the spread creates natural ripples and water action associated with dabbling. Another way to create realism is to have someone kick their feet back and forth in the water. While this works best if the individual is relatively close to the decoys, simply creating movement nearby is also effective.

The use of confidence decoys is considered a personal choice when pursuing timber ducks. It's my belief that they are unnecessary. Given the surrounding canopy, birds will be almost land-on-your-hat-close, so that added step really isn't necessary. In larger areas, it can be left up to the hunter's discretion.

Gadwalls are really not much different from other puddle species. They regularly decoy to a dozen blocks or so, and they love movement. Water depth plays a huge part in deciding if a timber hole is suitable gadwall habitat. The perfect gadwall depth is 8 to 10 feet (2.4 to 3 m). Not minding the longer dive, gadwalls are more apt to adapt to deeper conditions than the other species.

DIVERS

Less imaginative than the other sets and usually with fewer options, decoying divers requires less strategy and more preparation. Divers are found on lakes, ponds and, occasionally, larger rivers, rarely frequenting marshes unless breeding or pressured. They feed and raft on large tracts of open water. For the hunter not afraid of a little work, divers can create great gunning opportunities long after most puddle ducks have left for the season.

One challenge to hunting divers is the need for using an entirely different decoy spread. The majority of puddle duck decoys won't suffice for diver scenarios. While a few frugal hunters do successfully use lighter-colored puddle species decoys (pintail and widgeon) in hope of mimicking divers, most sportsmen learn to set a spread specifically for divers.

As an example, let's assume that a large flock of divers has been located feeding from a weed flat, several hundred yards (meters) from shore. They are not close enough to take advantage of any shore cover, requiring large-water methods.

Typically, divers feed daily on a single food source such as wild celery, until it's exhausted or weather drives them away. Hunting pressure can also influence diver movements, sending flocks farther south prematurely. Because the birds usually feed in water exceeding 20 feet (6 m), wading isn't possible; a boat or stilt blind must be used. I suggest you use two vessels—one for the actual travel and a smaller one to act as a blind. The second one can also be used to haul decoys or other heavy gear.

Decoying divers requires many hours of pre-hunt preparation. With water depths usually exceeding 20 feet (6 m) , main lines or "longlines" are needed to secure the decoy pattern. Rigged similar to the main lines described for puddlers in the river, lines will need to be much longer, and supplied with many more decoys. Although 12 to 18 decoys were sufficient for those smaller river scenarios, "diver lines" will require 24 decoys or more.

Usually, several dozen birds are commonly seen during later seasons. To portray this scenario, large fishhook, half-circle or half-moon patterns are required. Much larger than puddler patterns, the end of each line for divers should reach 60 to 70 yards (54.6 to 63.7 m) past the hidden hunters. Unlike puddlers, divers won't circle a spread, examining every inch. But rather, they lock in on one of the lines and follow it to the landing pocket located in the center. If the set is constructed correctly, the birds should land 20 to 30 yards (18.2 to 27.3 m) from the waiting hunters. Remember, spreads that have landing pockets too wide or deep lead the birds to land out of range.

Confidence decoys are rarely used when hunting divers. In most cases, hunters assume that deep water and the distance hunted from shore requires less disguise. However, I have found that placing some confidence decoys acts to neutralize a location, keeping it fresh and productive for many days to come. Confidence decoys for large-water sets include swans, coots, seagulls and geese. You will find that setting a small flock of seagulls, coots or geese will ward off any future decoy shyness.

Mechanical decoys are rarely utilized in diver hunting, but flagging is a popular strategy. Much like goose hunting, using a standard Canada goose flag should do the trick. Once flocks have committed, sit back and let them cruise down their chosen line. Divers are fast; don't forget to reload!

SEA DUCKS

These are some of the more physically demanding ducks to hunt. With temperatures usually at freezing or below, and with the propensity for rough seas, hunting sea ducks isn't for the faint of heart.

Flocking in large rafts, common sea species such as eiders, scoters, harlequins and long-tails spend the late fall and winter months feeding in deeper water on crustaceans and mollusks. Targeting this food source, usually near large rocky cliffs or islands, gives the hunter ample opportunities to create a realistic and stealthy spread.

For sea ducks, you need about 18 to 24 decoys matching the pursued bird. A spread of scoters usually also works in a pinch. With water depths being usually too deep to consider manually setting and collecting individual blocks, sea blocks are always attached to a main line and gang rigged (rigged multiple blocks to a line). Spaced from 4 to 8 feet (1.2 to 2.4 m) apart, the lines are next laid in a very loose grid or rafting pattern. Each main line is anchored with weights of 5 pounds (2.25 kg) or heavier, with the closest end sometimes tied to shore.

Remembering that, in general, sea ducks aren't very vocal and rarely plop down in the middle of a decoy spread, they offer the wingshooter great pass-shooting opportunities. Knowing their unlikely nature of jacking (quickly landing) into the spread, some form of motion will get them to take a longer look at your spread. As with freshwater diver species, flagging is an excellent choice here. Another alternative that works very well is using some form of mechanical floating decoy—spinning-wing designs are the best and quiver magnets or bubbler models also work nicely.

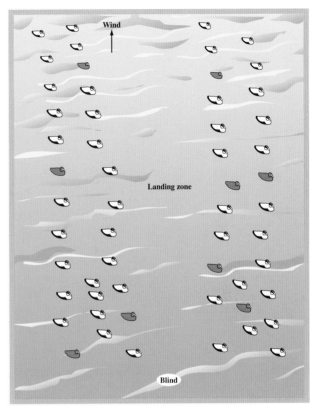

Attach a 5- to 10-pound anchor to the upwind end of each longline. Run lines on either side of the blind, leaving a 10- to 15-yard opening in the middle for a landing zone.

If you sit in the middle of the spread, the birds are usually out of range as they land. Instead, position yourself on the side of the spread where the ducks arrive from. Because these ducks usually dart across the spread before rafting to one side, a landing pocket is unnecessary. Place your blind on a shoreline, jetty or rocky outcropping, so you can use the natural topography, and try to blend in on either side of the decoys.

Always be aware of the tide and water levels when hunting these more dangerous locations. In a matter of minutes the landscape can change dramatically.

When targeting less-predictable flocks or during periods of higher water, you can use the same decoy rigging, but instead connect it to a boat's transom and then simply drif about. This method works well when trying to locate a feeding area or an acceptable outcropping to secure a spread. Usually, the ducks ignore the boat and dart across to take a look at the spread.

GEESE

Although some waterfowl experts argue that the differences in overall strategy between species is like night and day, I have found only slight differences that advanced goose hunters pay attention to. The overall strategy, setup and planning is almost identical. Whether you hunt geese on water or over feed fields the challenge will bring great rewards.

FIELD SETS

There's little difference between goose and puddler field decoying methods. Both require a knowledge of the land, proper positioning, many decoys and motion to be successful. Hunting puddle ducks over feed fields can seem like a timed parade, with heavy flights early in the morning and again later in the afternoon. A benefit of field hunting for geese accommodates the hunter who would prefer to hunt all day. Regardless of species, flocks of geese regularly spend the morning feeding in crop fields, leave during the early afternoon to grab a drink, and then return again until dark, making this style of goose hunting so productive. In areas with little to slight hunting pressure, the waterfowler can select birds while they travel to and from their destinations—all day long. That said, I still recommend that you also scout during the day. The knowledge of the area and experience with the flying patterns you gain will better prepare you for the next outing.

When first examining a proper goose field, it's important to differentiate between where the geese come from and where they go after feeding. It's frustrating to locate a well-used field loaded with geese, only to set up the next morning in the wrong section. Geese, like ducks, are creatures of habit, and this characteristic is good to keep in mind when decoying.

As with ducks, goose decoy patterns are dictated by the particular topography of the area. For a good example, let's assume that this field is several hundred acres (hectares) wide, by at least half as long. Geese have been entering this field northbound throughout most of the day and then returning southbound toward their roost at night. Tracks, droppings and feathers clearly mark the area where they are feeding. As with most other waterfowl hunting applications, the birds themselves generally tell the hunter what he or she has to do to be successful. Using the same principles discussed in the duck field section, the decoy spread should face toward the south in the morning, with the landing pocket open and facing the oncoming birds. Later in the day, the spread

should be repositioned with the opening faced toward the direction they return from.

If you plan to hunt all day, positioning the spread with two landing pockets (one in front and one in back) is the best overall method. Don't forget to include a spot for the blind close by. It can be on the edge of the pocket, as with the strategies for hunting puddlers in fields, or in some surrounding cover if available.

Spread selections are dictated by available decoy numbers and land topography. On average, the half-moon works well for this scenario. If more decoys are available, a half-circle can be used. Individual decoy placement is also very important. Remember that geese live in small family groups. These groups usually don't include more than four to ten birds, though some larger groups have been documented. Like laying the proper positioning for the spread shape, setting each individual decoy in some form of a grouping pattern is necessary. Use 4 to 6 decoys for the best result. Almost any decoy design works—shell, full body, silhouette, etc.

Snows and Blues. Decoy selection varies from species to species. In some instances a particular species requires some form of special catering to ensure a quality hunt. For instance, when creating spreads for snow and blues, decoy numbers will have to be ten times larger than any Canada or specklebelly spread.

To achieve such a large spread, rag decoys numbering in the hundreds are necessary to pull large migrating flocks from the sky. To add realism and depth to this spread, use several dozen shell decoys mixed with silhouettes. Snow geese need to see that there are plenty of other birds in order for them to land. Kites, flags or windsocks will also add movement and variety. Large grounded flocks of snows or blues will always have at least some members waddling around in search of food, making kites, windsocks or flags mandatory. If you add a small flock of specklebellies or Canadas as confidence decoys, be prepared to shoot!

Canadas. Living and traveling in much smaller flocks, Canada spreads should include fewer birds—two to six dozen decoys. In the following example, four to six dozen decoys are needed because the field is rather large. Successful decoy choices are the more lifelike styles such as silhouettes, shells and full-bodied. With fewer decoys required, even the traveling hunter can afford to employ more full-bodieds and shells, rather than rags or lighter inflatables.

Spread choice should ultimately be half-moon or half-circle shapes. There really isn't any other practical alternative if the spread is based in the middle of the field. Individual decoy positioning is especially important, as Canadas tend to be more social birds. Movement for a Canada spread is important, but not to the degree it is with snow geese. By using far fewer decoys, the hunter is only obligated to mimic a smaller percentage of movement. Mechanicals work well in Canada spreads; flagging works best, as the movement can be more easily controlled, and employed upon the first sight of a flock.

White-Fronteds. These geese have nearly identical decoy and spread requirements as Canadas. Positioning, spread types and decoy models are very similar. In fact, using Canada decoys for specks has been the answer for many waterfowlers in a pinch. One major difference is in decoy numbers. While the majority of today's speck spreads are made with about 12 decoys, many southern hunters utilize only two, three or four. Known as being very species oriented, white-fronted geese are easily attracted to just a few decoys, if the conditions are correct. When setting a spread in a large feeding scenario, at least a dozen decoys is the recommended number.

Hunting geese on water requires the same overall knowledge and presentation as hunting them on land. However, most land-hunting scenarios position the hunter to decoy and shoot birds coming to feed. Hunting on water is quite different. Birds use water continually–every day–drinking, feeding and roosting on it. When water hunting, the goal is to know enough about the geese's normal routine to either hide in ambush or adjust the decoy strategy.

For this scenario, let's assume that the area that's being hunted is a large lake. Typically, there is very little cover or topographical variety, but the hunter must still create a realistic spread. Of course, if the area closely bordered a field or marsh, more options would be available to the hunter.

Examining the scene, the first questions that should be asked and answered are: Why are the geese arriving in this location? And at what time does goose activity commence? When hunting larger sections of water, most goose activity will be based on their requirement for water after feeding. While geese may be seen dabbling while on the water body, their goal is to quench their thirst. Consequently, this activity is usually seen later in the morning or during the early afternoon, once they have finished feeding.

Another strategy for decoying lies in intercepting flocks during their main travel patterns. These are geese that may have roosted in a nearby shallow bay or marsh and are using the lake as an interim stop to feeding grounds. Once the fly routine is discovered, be it a simple travel route, or a post-feeding water schedule, the hunting can seem simple.

Most water spreads for geese are straightforward, with the use of a common pattern. In this case, a half-moon or raft design are the best choices. Assuming the hunter has chosen this location for both an early-season hunt as well as a last-week adventure, each pattern fits a certain timeframe.

In early to mid-October, when geese are still quite comfortable to land and feed in and among different hunted areas, geese will rarely display any raft-ing behavior. Freely swimming and feeding, the half-moon pattern, with the landing pocket in the center, is the best choice. Later, when geese have survived the first few weeks of intense pressure, or are arriving in an area as migrants, their body language is most apt to display larger rafting tendencies. Knowing there is safety in numbers, geese swim and rest much closer to each other, with hopes of blending in. There is usually very little room for others to land, but rather, incoming geese create another raft nearby. Creating either type of spread is easy, with the right equipment.

For an early-season set, use singly rigged blocks placed in a half-moon pattern around the boat. This layout uses the decoys to break up the vessel's silhouette, while also suggesting that the swimming "geese" are comfortable around the foreign object. Geese won't try if they don't feel comfortable. For this early-season set, 12 to 24 decoys best mimic a flock of "local" birds.

Later in the season, when luring migrants or heavily pressured birds, employing main lines with many decoys is necessary. While two dozen sufficed for the early season strategy, four dozen or more blocks connected to three or four main lines is the best bet when creating a raft. Remember, the main lines must be positioned close enough to insinuate a tight group. Placing your boat in the middle, or at one end (depending on what direction the geese are mainly traveling from) puts you in the best position for the shot. If hunting with another vessel, creating two rafts and then positioning the boat between them, with a small opening in the center, is another excellent way to fool geese. The added realism of double the number of decoys may be enough to draw down a flock, if only for a quick look.

While movement in and around a field flock can be great, water flocks will require much less movement to get their attention, as the their main focus is to drink and rest. Employing a quiver magnet or two among the decoys creates just enough water movement that the birds won't look like decoys.

Remember: If hunting the late season, migrants have seen almost every trick in the book, so be sure to mimic what the birds are currently doing, and not what's being done by surrounding hunters. Early-season endeavors may call for a spinning-wing, or mechanical water set to produce a response. The Mojo Goose, coupled with flagging, works well for this application.

Confidence decoys for a goose-hunting application is the exact opposite of hunting ducks over water. When looking for the best and most realistic confidence decoy, using a dozen or two of the most common duck species is a great choice. Exactly like any other confidence spread, position them to one side of the intended species, preferably not on the side that the geese are expected to come from. If the area has seen this "duck" trick, setting a small flock of coots or seagulls is another alternative.

CHAPTER SEVEN

Calling Puddle Ducks

Like learning to play a musical instrument, calling waterfowl requires learning some basic skills, then having time to perfect them. It's one of the most difficult aspects of waterfowling for anyone to master, but the rewards are great.

Waterfowl calls are available in two styles: single reed and double reed. As the names imply, single-reed calls employ just one reed, while double-reed calls use two. The differences are found in volume and air pressure. The original call on the market, the single reed, is designed for loud, long-range calling. Requiring more air pressure when blowing, the single reed is usually used by more-experienced callers.

The double reed is more beginner friendly, requiring less air pressure when blowing, and offering a wider range of sounds. It's the best choice for any novice. Quieter and softer in tone, the double reed isn't recommended for the louder hail calls, or where heavy volume is needed.

Thanks in part to the fact that the majority of puddle species are very social, and that the mallard call is relatively close in context to many others, seventy-five percent of all puddler calling is based almost entirely on the vocabulary of the mallard. This is why you see mainly mallard calls used so often—particularly mallard hen calls. The quacking, feeding chatter and hailing of the mallard hen is mainly used. A much smaller fraction of calling from the drake is ever utilized.

In a nutshell, here's the proper way to hold a common mallard duck call: Gripping the lower sound trough with the index finger and thumb, loosely wrap the rest of the hand around the lower section of the call, creating a "bell," or sound pocket. It's important to have this barricade separating and re-directing the sound from the outside of the barrel. It's with this hand control that you can manipulate the call and better create authentic sounds. Once you understand hand placement, mastering the basic notes is the next challenge.

When callers first begin, many believe that they must blow as hard as they possibly can in order to get any fowl-like sound. They quickly find that harsh calling like this only tires them out and possibly dislodges the reed from the assembly. Calling is done correctly by growling or grunting into the call. Simply blowing the call, especially without any control over the caller's breathing, creates only a hollow, non-duck sound.

If you are lucky enough to have an experienced caller help you, or you invest in one of the quality calling DVDs or cads, you will see that calling any waterfowl requires great breath control as well as a knowledge of notes and note combinations.

Creating notes and maintaining proper air pressure can be done in one of two methods: The first is to collect air and then disperse it at the appropriate time through the assistance of the caller's diaphragm. Utilizing the diaphragm while calling any species affords the caller the ability to growl and grunt and create more authentic sounds. The second is to say a word sound into the call. This is how the most basic notes are created. This technique is also helpful when trying to control airflow, but is mainly used to produce the proper note sounds. Best yet, if the caller can comfortably do it, is to combine the two forms.

Hold the stopper between your thumb and forefinger.

Clean your call by pulling it apart and running cold water between the reed and tone board.

Use a double lanyard on one call to prevent losing the stopper.

The first notes to learn are the basic quack and cluck. They are created by saying the actual words QUACK, WICK, KAK and WHAT (personal preference and call design will dictate which ones work best). When spoken into the call, these four words create the basic quacking and clucking sounds on which the entire vocabulary is built. Once you find a particular word or sound to be the most realistic choice for the particular call, spend some time practicing this simple call. Adequately knowing how to quack will lay the framework for other, more difficult notes and calls.

Another basic note is the TICK or TICK-IT sounds. These are most easily done by actually saying the word TICK, or PUT. These words eventually create the feeding and flying chatter that will build the basis of a calling sequence. Once the basic TICK is learned, the novice caller has enough knowledge to begin to study the following half-dozen common calls that are used when puddler hunting.

Hail Call

This is the attention-getting call used when first working a string of birds. Rarely used when hunting small areas such as flooded timber or small marshes, it's the combination of many drawn-out quacks that are high in the first few notes, while continually being drawn out. After three or four long notes, the last five or six notes are sped up at the end of the sequence. Loud, drawn-out and usually very clear, this call has little purpose except to draw attention to a spread. One note: When hunting highly pressured areas or later in the season, a hail call can flair (disperse) ducks as fast as it can attract them. When done correctly, a hail call can be represented like this:

QU……ACK- QU……ACK- QU……ACK-
QU….ACK- QU….ACK- QU…ACK- QU..ACK-
QU..ACK- QUACK.

The dots between the first and second section of the note represent the approximate time that each note or half note should be held. Usually overdone in most marshes, you can hear an example by simply listen to surrounding blinds. This is almost always the first call used when beginning a sequence.

A great choice for a ringing hail call is Primos single-reed acrylic contender, which blows wet or dry, and is incredibly loud.

Cluck

This is a single quack made when the hen is content or happily communicating with others; usually heard between swimming birds. Used by hunters as a method to mimic many birds, the cluck is made by saying WACK or KAK into the call in one short burst. Relatively low in volume, this is a great finishing call to supplement a routine between feeding chatter and laydown calls.

Lone Hen Call

This basic call is usually heard early in the morning to reassemble a roosted flock before a takeoff. It is also used late in the evening to locate nearby birds. Created by saying QU....ACK-KAK-KAK-KAK-QU....ACK-QU....ACK, this basic mini-sequence works well if used periodically throughout the day as a contented confidence call. Another popular use is during the late season, or when pursuing highly pressured birds. It's rarely used in a regular calling sequence.

Laydown Call

Also called the landing call, it is primarily used when coaxing birds the last few yards to your decoys. A four- or five-note call, it can be heard when a flock of ducks is contentedly landing among other birds. Best reproduced by saying QUACK or WICK four or five times, all the notes begin on a higher pitch and then rapidly drop to lower notes: WICK-wick-wick-wick.

Don't confuse this vocalization with the faster, more drawn out and almost flat-noted quacking of an alerted or frightened puddler. Usually this ruckus is heard when the birds are alarmed and lifting off the water or flying away from danger. The landing call should never be reproduced at this faster pace or with flat, staccato notes. A common mistake is made when the caller becomes excited and moves the call in several directions, as if trying to redirect the volume. The call ends up sounding like a warning–not a good idea! Learning to make this call correctly takes practice–to adjust the rise and fall in pitch and get the proper speed. Don't become frustrated; it comes with time and practice.

Feeding Call

Also called the feeding chuckle or the flight chuckle, this is a multi-noted call that is extremely easy to reproduce. The basic form is executed by saying TICK-TICK-TICK-TICK-TICK-TICK or PUT-PUT-PUT-PUT-PUT-PUT into the call.

Once this can be completed with very little lag time, adding "IT" to the notes makes the complete forms: TICK-IT,TICK-IT,TICK,TICK-IT,TICK, TICK-IT, TICK-TICK or PUT-IT, PUT-IT, PUT-IT, PUT-IT, PUT-IT, PUT-IT. Any difference between the versions is in their application.

The feeding chuckle is used when adding realism to a regular calling sequence. This call is also appropriate when using a jerk cord or other mechanical decoy when working oncoming birds.

The flight chuckle is primarily used when birds are communicating in flight. Sounding much like the feeding chuckle, the main difference is in the total number of combined notes. Requiring fewer notes, the flight chuckle is based on a four-note combination. When done correctly it resembles TICK-TICK-IT, TICK-IT, TICK.

Both chuckles should be blown semi-fast to fast. Regardless of the exact note count or pace, these calls should mimic contented birds either flying in to feed, roost or rest, or birds that are already feeding. Using an averaged-size spread in conjunction with these calls allows the hunter to represent the entire flock of comfortable birds.

Comeback Call

Used as the last effort when the birds have semi-committed before starting to leave. It is very productive when birds are likely to land outside of the landing pocket. It can also be used as a filler in a calling sequence.

Similar to the hail call or lone hen, it's a six- or seven-note call that is formed by saying QUACK-QUACK-QUACK-QU…ACK-QU….ACK-QU……ACK.

Related closely to the hail, it starts quickly and ends with steadily longer, drawn-out notes. Unlike the hail call, this call should be of continuously normal volume. If the birds aren't responding, the volume should be steadily intensified until the birds come back into range or leave completely. You may want to stop this call if birds aren't cooperating. While it may lose its realistic qualities, it gains the attention-grabbing component of the hail.

Call Combinations

Putting these individual calls into practice, you can create and modify many different calling routines. Using the ever changing variables of weather, local hunting pressure, a particular duck's response and topography, you must create an appropriate sequence. When first trying duck calling, it's best to begin with a standard routine and steadily modify it to your particular quarry. Here's an example of such a routine:

QU……ACK-QU……ACK-QU……ACK-QU….ACK-QU…ACK-QU..ACK-QUACK-KAK-KAK-TICK-TICK-TICK-IT-TICK-TICK-IT-TICK-IT-TICK-IT-TICK-IT-KAK-KAK-WICK-WICK-WICK-WICK.

If the birds have come near your spread, circled the decoys and are now starting back away from the spread, add this:

QUACK-QUACK-QUACK-QU…ACK-QU…..ACK-QU……ACK.

If they haven't come back into range after working them this far, you may as well look for others. Not all birds respond to a call and decoy spread as you would like them to. Possibly because of extreme hunting pressure or the fact that they may have another agenda, birds sometimes pass right by without even a look. It's not always something you did incorrectly, but quite often just a random, natural response. Of course, if you are posted in the wrong location, this "phenomenon" is just poor planning.

When trying to mimic other hen mallard vocabulary, it's best to employ a double reed. It requires less effort to blow and it's usually easier to create the gravely duck-like sounds. An excellent choice is the Primos Pro Mallard; equipped with a two-reed system and a tuning hole, it's great for creating the illusion of multiple ducks.

If you encounter a larger ratio of teal, wood ducks, pintails or gadwalls to mallards, they readily travel to mallard calling, but not in all circumstances. Roosting in small quasi flocks, wood ducks peep and whistle to communicate, before lifting at daybreak. Green-winged teal not only quack, but the drakes peep in short bursts. And one can't forget the buzzing sound of the drake mallard.

WOOD DUCKS

Not able to make a quacking sound, wood ducks use two distinct whistle-type calls to communicate. The peep sounds a lot like a young chick. It is primarily used when contentedly communicating on the water while feeding or during pre-dawn, just before lifting.

Creating this call is much like blowing a dog whistle in short bursts. There is no need to say any words or word sounds into the call, but rather simply blow it. A common sequence may sound like PEEP, PEEP PEEPPEEP, PEEP, PEEPPEEP. This sequence is best when trying to work pre-dawn woodies that haven't left the seclusion of the marsh yet.

Another common sound in the wood duck's vocabulary is the whistle. Every waterfowler has heard this call if they have spent any time at all in the marsh. Sounding almost identical to the low-to-high-note draw of a child's slide whistle, it begins on a low note and ends high. If diagramed, it would look something like PaaaeeeeeeEEEEEP. This is a very rough rendition, but you get the idea.

The use of this call is dictated by both the time of day and the duck's particular feeling. Also utilizing this sound when first leaving their roost sites, wood ducks give one or two long whistles. Expecting an answer, the birds use this as a form of pre-flight communication. Once daylight is visible, the birds make the same whistle call when dabbling or swimming about, usually when trying to locate other woodies.

If in danger or about to lift out of fright, a bird makes the same whistle three to five times very fast, in repetition. You don't want to hear this call. It usually signifies that the hunter prematurely bumped the birds while arriving, or the birds have seen something that's troubling.

To utilize wood duck calls, whether for confidence calling for other species or when pursuing wood ducks, you should either blow peeps or single whistles. Never blow three or more whistles in a single sequence, as this will push away ducks of either species, rather than pull them in.

GREEN-WINGED TEAL

A sound that's common, especially during the early season, is the peep of the drake green-winged teal. Usually heard when in a flock, teal peeps are a welcomed addition to any puddle spread. Signifying contentment, the call can be employed as a filler, while another hunter uses mallard calls. Or, it can be used on its own when coaxing teal the last few yards (meters) to the decoys.

The hunter should blow four to seven short quick peeps in staccato, almost identical to the pitch of the wood duck peep. The correct sequence can look like this:

Manufacturers such as Cass Creek Game Calls offer a full line of electronic call options.

PEEP-PEEPPEEP-PEEP-PEEP-PEEPPEEPPEEP-PEEP

An inexpensive, yet very effective call for both teal and wood ducks is the Haydel's MP-90 Magnum Pintail. Very effective on pintails and drake mallards, the MP-90 easily makes the peeps and whistles of both the wood ducks and teal. Extremely small, it and can be attached to the base of any lanyard.

NORTHERN PINTAIL

Teal and wood ducks aren't the only ducks to use some form of vocabulary other than a quack. Drake pintails use a form of whistle as well. The drake, when communicating both in the air and on water, whistles in short bursts, while sounding like he's rolling his tongue. Done correctly, it sounds similar to an English police whistle: PEEP-PEEEEP-PEEP.

Blowing in the same fashion as for the teal peep, you must add a flutter of the tongue or roll the throat to achieve the rolling characteristics. Start with regular mallard calling and then gradually work in the rolling whistle as the final invitation.

MALLARD DRAKE

Used as a supplement when calling both mallards and other puddle species, the mallard whistle is easy to make. The drake "hum" or "buzz" is correctly made by humming in short bursts into the call. If illustrated, it looks like HMMM-HMMM-HMMM.

The mallard drake whistle is not only effective for all species, it's also a great call to teach children, as it can be learned quickly—and mistakes are hardly recognized.

The Primos High Roller whistle is blown similarly to any other waterfowl whistle, but incorporates a built-in roller. The call automatically flutters when air is blown through it. Also, employing tuning holes, the hunter can blow drake mallard calls (without the flutter) as well as sound like two different pintails.

GADWALL

This species also responds very well to mallard lingo, as the two hens sound similar. Beginning each gadwall sequence with mallard hen vocabulary is not only realistic, but also a great attention-getting call when working a flock. The hen gadwall's vocabulary can be made on almost any mallard call. Softer, nasal quacks, usually consisting of three or four notes are the majority of the hen's vocabulary. The males, while they don't make a quack or quack-like sound, actually say TAT. Like the vocalizations of the drake teal, the TAT is blown with the same cadence. Illustrated it looks like this:

TAT-TA-TAT-TAT-TAT.

A great call for precisely mimicking both the hen and drake gadwall sounds is the Haydel's Gadwall G-W-01. It produces the perfect nasal quacks that are needed to draw birds in close.

Calling Geese

Gaining the foundation necessary to be a competent goose caller won't come overnight. The challenge of learning not only the individual species vocabularies, but also the necessary techniques for each call can seem overwhelming. But with a step-by-step approach, it all can be mastered.

For geese, there are two basic call types: the flute and the short reed. Creating the ghostly moans and clucks associated with a longer call barrel, the flute is a great beginner's choice for creating rudimentary goose sounds. To learn an expanded version of a goose vocabulary, use the short reed. Made popular over the past few years, short-reed calls require more breath control, yet afford the caller the ability to create a slightly more realistic sequence. Richie McKnight, Knight & Hale's on-staff goose-calling champion stresses that short-reed sounds are best produced with breath control and elaboration, versus using the traditional "tonguing" or tongue manipulation that is usually employed. While the use of the caller's diaphragm and breathing take more time and practice to master, Richie guarantees a cleaner, more gooselike quality, no matter what the call.

Regardless of the call's design, creating realistic goose sounds requires the use of both hands. Correct hand positioning is (if you're right handed) with the right thumb and forefinger cupped in a small circle. The first joint of the thumb and the first joint of the forefinger (from the nail down) should gently lay on top of one another. Having the thumb resting on the forefinger creates a valve-like opening for the ball of the call to fit into. This controls the air space necessary to achieve proper sound. The left hand should be slightly cupped and rested heel-to-heel against the right hand. This creates a "bell" or sound chamber, much like the opening in a guitar box. The bell section of the call fits in between the caller's hands. Through opening and closing this chamber, the caller can make resonating or flat tones.

When first learning to call geese, don't be afraid or embarrassed to puff out your cheeks for the proper breathing techniques necessary for success. Unlike duck calling, goose calling doesn't require the use of the diaphragm or throat. But rather, you blow through a goose call much like blowing up a beach ball or balloon. It's important to keep the tongue at the base of the mouth. This makes a larger air cavity, especially important when blowing a short reed. If the cavity is too small, air is forced into the call at too high a pressure and you "squeak," rather than call a note.

While there are literally hundreds of goose calls on the market, the Knight and Hale Richie McKnight series Long Honker Goose Flute is one of the better calls for the novice and experienced alike. For the hunter searching for a short-reed call, the Richie McKnight Pit Magic and Pit Boss are good choices.

CANADA GOOSE

As with the basics of duck calling, there are note sounds, or words, that the caller can say to achieve the exact vocalization. Depending on style of call, these notes or word sounds can have a large range.

Hail Call

As in duck calling, this call is designed to grab the attention of a distant flock, even as far as 300 to 400 yards (273 to 364 m) away. Very loud and simple, the hail has this sole purpose. Illustrated, the hail looks like:

TUUUUUUU-WIT, TUUUUUUU-WIT, TUUUUUUU-WIT.

Blown with the first TU extended, it can sound at first like something of a moan. The hail should be blown with small pauses between notes. This by no means is an excited call but, like the lost call, is designed to turn heads.

After holding the first TU to the count of five, the caller must next blow a faster burst of air, while still blowing the original TU. This is called "breaking the reed." It's the speed and amount of air blown through the call that will make it "break," or go from a low note to a high note. This call is the base upon which all other goose vocalizations are built.

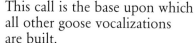

Manufacturers such as Haydel's Game Calls, Hunter's Specialties and Buck Gardner Calls offer full lines of good call choices.

Greeting Call

This call is blown much faster and used when the geese are interested in the decoy spread and seem to want a closer look. It simulates a flock of contentedly feeding geese that are happy to see the incoming flock. This call uses the TU-WIT clucks from the hail call, but drastically shortens them and mixes the cadence. Illustrated, the greeting looks like:

TU-WIT, TU-WIT, WIT, TU, TU-WIT, WIT-WIT, TU-WIT TU-TU, WIT.

This would be the advanced model of the greeting call. The novice could simply blow a TU-WIT combination, only changing the cadence, and be successful.

Laydown Call

This is a series of clucks and occasional honks that replicate birds both feeding or preparing to land. Identical to the pulsating vocalizations of an angry bear, the laydown call is best mimicked by saying DO-DO-DO-DO-DO-DO-DO-DO. Make sure that this note is blown in one steady stream, so the reed doesn't break from the original DUUR-RRRRRRR or BUURRRRRRRRR sound. Blown with an alternating cadence, the laydown should start fast, go slow and then fast again. Some hunters continue this cadence, but I have found this to be overdone and unnatural. Mixing cadences more closely creates the essence of an actual flock.

Once the base of the laydown call is learned, you should add the occasional honk or yodel. An advanced laydown sequence would look something like this:

DO-DO-DO-DO-DO; then a fast TU-WIT; another DO-DO-DO-DO; and a slower TU-WIT, TU-WIT, DO-DO-DO.

If for some reason the flock fades out of gun range on a breeze, or they suddenly veer to one side, you need to use the comeback call.

Comeback Call

This is used when the geese are leaving. It pulls birds back even after the first shots are fired. Mesmerized by the pleading nature of this call, geese forget their detour route and come back for a closer look. Illustrated, the call looks like this:

TU-WIIIIIIIIIIIIIIT, TU-WIIIIIIIIIIIIIIT, TU-WIIIIIIIIIIIIIIIIIT.

Relatively close to the high ending of a wood duck call, the end of the honk is blown so that it ends on a high note. This call usually requires a great deal of practice, as it requires lots of air just to start the note combination. Then, because of its high inflection, the caller must find even more air to complete it. Once the basic call is mastered, you will become fast enough to take a breath in between calls, and have plenty of air to the end.

Occasionally geese arrive solo or, if their mate is lost during the first few shots, they circle continuously overhead, with hope of reconnecting. While the comeback call does work in this situation, the lost call works even better.

Lost Call

Used not only when working a solo goose, the lost call can be used as a sequence supplement. It is also successful on smaller flocks of three or four birds. It looks like this:

TUUUUUUUUUUUU-WAA,
TUUUUUUUUUUUU-WAA,
TUUUUUUUUUUUU-WAA.

Yodel

This is a fast, low-to-high sound that takes most novices many hours to perfect. Used by geese when very excited, it's imitated by very quickly saying TU-TU-WIT, TU-TU-WIT, TU-TU-WIT into the call. When done at the perfect speed, this three-note vocalization blends into a single-note call with differing inflections, actually sounding like yodeling.

Double-Cluck

This is another advanced vocalization to use if other hunters in the area aren't using it. Made by saying TU-WIT-A, the average sequence would look like this:

TU-WIT-A TU-WIT-A TU-WIT-A.

Blown very fast, the three notes blend as with a yodel, and form a "TWITA" sound. It's often heard when geese are excitedly landing, especially when landing near other geese.

SEQUENCES

Similar to duck calling, creating a goose sequence is the first step in finding a successful and reliable routine. Below is the sequence I use most often when working "Cans" from start to finish. For this example, let's assume that the birds have arrived in the typical nature. I begin with the hail call and progress through the rest of the vocalizations. Shots are fired and I am trying to bring the last few back to me. A six-step approach that works anywhere looks similar to this:

Step 1. TUUUUUUUU-WIT, TUUUUUUU-WIT,TUUUUUUUU-WIT

Step 2. TU-WIT,TU-WIT,WIT,TU, TU-WIT, WIT-WIT, TU-WIT TU-TU, WIT

Step 3. TU-TU-WIT, TU-TU-WIT, TU-TU-WIT––TU-WIT-A TU-WIT-A TU-WIT-A

Step 4. TU-WIT,TU-WIT,WIT,TU, TU-WIT, WIT-WIT, TU-WIT TU-TU, WIT

Step 5. DO-DO-DO-DO-DO (fast) TU-WIT, DO-DO-DO-DO (slower) TU-WIT, TU-WIT, DO-DO-DO

Step 6. TU-WIIIIIIIIIIIIIIT, TU-WIIIIIIIIIIIIIIIIT, TU-WIIIIIIIIIIIIIIIIT––TUUUUUUUUUUUUU-WAA–– TUUUUUUUUUUUU-WAA, TUUUUUUUUUUUU-WAA

These techniques work equally well with a short-reed style of call. Trading TU for WHO and TU-WIT for WHOOO-IT is all that is necessary to apply these same concepts to a short-reed call. Well, that and a lot of practice.

SNOW AND BLUE GEESE

Calling snow geese and their blue-phase cousins is very different from calling Canadas.

While Cans have a specific language and vocalizations, snows have a language, but the differentiation between vocalizations can become fuzzy. Flocking in groups of several hundred birds to several thousand, calling isn't nearly as important to hunting snows as it is to hunting Canadas. Usually, success is based on a huge decoy spread and pre-hunt scouting. That said, it's true that snows are callable. When small groups of birds break from the main flock, or if singles or pairs arrive, calling to these sometimes lost, or isolated birds will almost definitely bring them in. Haydel's SN-04 Snow Goose Call is an excellent choice.

Similar to preparations for calling Canadas, position the call between thumb and index finger of your dominant hand. Wrap the other hand over it, creating a "bell," or sound chamber. (This sound chamber strategy is also used when calling specks.)

Two notes are commonly used with snows and blues: the cluck and the yodel.

Cluck

The cluck is a single-note vocalization that geese use when alone, in pairs or in triples. Commonly heard when birds are communicating with other birds that have already landed, the number of clucks used by the approaching birds dictates how many the caller should make. If, for example, the birds are using two-note clucks, then the caller should use two notes as well.

To form a cluck, purse your lips and simply huff into the call. No word sounds are necessary. This simple sound is a basic cluck. Combining two or three clucks in a sequence will match the most common snow-calling sequence.

Yodel

Created by combining multiple clucks in a fast cadence. Many callers find it easier to flutter their tongue while blowing the initial cluck. This may make it easier to achieve the required note connection. The yodel is often heard when geese are rallying to and from the ground.

WHITE-FRONTED GEESE

As with snow geese, successfully calling white-fronteds, or specklebellies, requires only a general knowledge of their vocabulary, which is built on the cluck system. Most speck calls are held and blown the same as snow calls, with clucks creating the general language and yodels filling in the void. Haydel's SP-04 Speck Call is the easiest I have found to blow and consistently obtain realistic yodels and clucks. Plus, it requires less back pressure than its competitors.

Unlike with Canada geese, specklebellies require calling right up until the first shots are fired. Unlike with snows or Canadas, where calling can cease and allow the birds to glide in, speck calling is done much faster and continuously.

Another key concept for calling white-fronted geese is the need to mimic exactly what the birds are doing. If a bird shows interest in the spread, and is using a two-note call, it's the caller's next move to immediately mimic their calling, as if trying to "out-call" the goose.

Rod Haydel discovered this technique decades ago, and the benefits are clearly seen when carrying out a stringer of prize specks. He has documented the consistency of unsuccessfully calling birds with a three-note sequence. It's not known why a three-note bird is almost always uncooperative. But Rod has found that mimicking the three-note call and then listening for the switch to a two-note response is usually proof positive that the bird can be swayed. If the goose doesn't make this change, it's usually best to look for another target.

Carlson Championship Calls (far left) and Haydel's Game Calls offer a variety of effective models.

CHAPTER NINE

Hunting Strategies

All waterfowl species have great visual acuity. That means in order to become a successful hunter you must accomplish four things: know your hunting area, be able to keep your position undetected, match your method to the situation and gather your downed birds efficiently. Each component depends on others to make your outing a success!

SCOUTING

As the old saying goes, successful hunters set their decoys where the birds are, not where they want them to be. Waterfowling requires a great deal of pre-hunt knowledge before heading afield. It does the hunter little good to hunt an area where the birds refuse to land or fly over. Some of the best methods used by successful waterfowlers are kin to scouting for other game. Looking, listening and viewing the quarry are all important aspects.

Making good use of pre-season scouting trips is a key component to successful waterfowling. This may include using binoculars ("glassing") in feed fields at dawn and dusk to pinpoint a hot location. It may mean arriving near a water body to listen for different vocalizations. Or it could include walking the area in search of bird droppings or tracks. Many hunters use some combination of all these strategies.

Once the presence of birds has been verified, don't forget that scouting also requires knowing the land or water. Waterfowl of all species use land forms as guides when flying. Tree lines, points, fence lines, roadways and other major land forms guide birds to and from their destinations. Taking a day or two to learn which path the birds use will save countless headaches later, when trying to pattern birds that have already arrived.

If your scouting indicates the geese may land on property that you are not familiar with, be sure to seek permission to hunt there before proceeding. Asking permission not only soothes landowners' worries of strange traffic or unwarranted visitors, but also gives hunters a good reputation.

If permission is given, all you need do is wait for the birds to leave and then assemble a blind or dig a pit for the next morning. If permission is denied, continue to watch the flock to learn where the birds end up after dark. If the roost site is located, it's quite possible you can intercept the birds through pass-shooting or jump-shooting even before the flock leaves the roost. Even if the flock becomes wise to the hunting pressure after several attempts, you usually get at least a few successful days before the flock leaves the area.

Through scouting you will be able to quickly form a game plan in similar situations, when variables aren't in your favor. Common waterfowling is based on connecting the dots between known and unknown variables. The more constants one has, the less experimental the outing.

STAYING HIDDEN

If there is one aspect that is even more vital than decoys or effective calling, it's staying unnoticed. If there is a facet of proper waterfowling that hunters seem to miss, it's knowing how to be concealed. For many, keeping a low profile while hunting can seem like an all-day chore. It's quite common during the early seasons to see novice waterfowlers standing unsheltered and exposed on an open point or water edge, merely wishing that the birds will fly within range. To their disappointment this rarely happens, and it's the hunters who have taken the steps to remain hidden who bag their limits.

Unlike with some big-game species, where the hunter can remain in the open as long as he or she stays still, ducks and geese rely on their aerial vision to spot waiting or approaching danger. The pattern of circles that a flock of birds flies when committing to a set of decoys isn't an accident. They are checking the surrounding area for danger, before taking the gamble of landing. And their vision is exceptional!

Natural Cover

More often than not, the materials needed to disappear are right at the hunter's fingertips. While this method may not be the best or most effective for blending in, certain scenarios demand this style of camouflage.

For example, hunting a goose refuge in Addison, Vermont, several years ago, I came upon a large pine that grew along the inside corner of a small bay. From the tracks and goose droppings along the shore and exposed sandbar, it was apparent that birds were using this section of water as a resting and drinking area before returning to the crop fields and unhuntable section of refuge to feed. Laying a medium-size combination land-and-water spread, I tucked myself back against the bull pine. By resting my back against the trunk, the large swooping branches afforded me excellent cover, while also allowing a small opening for my shot. The afternoon came, and with it several snows that fell victim to my hidden position.

Returning the next weekend, I arrived at the pine to find that another hunter had cut all the branches and merely leaned against the tree for a shot—as a cigarette butt marked the location. Wishing I had now brought one of my portable blinds, I had no choice but to sit in the same position and hope that my camouflage clothing would suffice.

Within minutes the birds arrived. Jacking in from several hundred yards (meters) away, as they had done the week earlier, they set their wings and prepared to land. Gliding for the last 100 yards (91 m), the snows suddenly swung sharply to their left and landed several hundred yards (meters) out of gun range. They had obviously spotted me—I never took such a chance again!

Other common options that present themselves are using bulrushes, swamp grass or cattails to mask your location. These species of vegetation work well when standing just inside the perimeter, lying among them in a sink box, or wading among them in deeper water. Trimming only the bare minimum for seeing and shooting is key, as the birds will quickly notice a bald spot. And if the action is fast and furious, an eye-level swath will rapidly appear from the muzzle blast, quickly ruining your hiding spot.

Natural cover doesn't have to be only aquatic vegetation. Quite often, especially when pass shooting during the later seasons, woody shoreline vegetation works well to conceal you. When hunting flooded timber, hunters can merely take a post among the trees and branch debris. This affords them the benefit of staying mobile and packing-in only the bare minimum of equipment.

Remember that camouflage patterns must be adapted to the new surroundings. The early-season hunter, who was once knee-deep in cattails and wearing marsh-type camo clothing, must now employ some form of woodland pattern.

Above-Ground Blind

Using a waterfowl blind requires the same principles as when hunting natural cover: The hunter must not only conceal his or her position, but not damage any surrounding cover. Usually, better blinds are built from the vegetation that matches the surrounding species, but is cut from another location.

The overall design and construction is relatively simple. It's important to create a base, whether an above-water platform (to stand on) or simply four posts (to drive a boat or canoe into). For either type, the base should be secure and stable. Using cedar posts as main supports is an excellent choice as they are inexpensive and blend well with most surroundings.

The next step is to fasten the sides. Most commonly used is chicken wire, as the builder can weave the natural vegetation through the openings for realism, while still affording a comfortable and spacious structure. Some hunters go so far as assembling a roof and other comforts. Of course, your choices will be made depending on available resources and time.

Pit Blind

In addition to building an above-ground blind, there are other, more stealthy options. Pit blinds with a roof that are dug into the ground are able to hide hunters perfectly below ground level. Hunters either sit or stand under the roof and then pop up when birds are within range. These are very common among larger waterfowling clubs or leases where they can be created and left in place indefinitely. Annually, crop fields are planted surrounding several pits. Depending on goose activity, hunters choose the pit in the best location.

One note: Many states have outlawed this type of structure. Be sure the state that's being hunted allows it.

Sink Box

Another stealthy approach is to construct a sink box, which is placed in the water and the hunter uses the available water depth as the ultimate concealment. Simply, a large garbage can or barrel is weighted down and hunters nestle themselves inside. This option is often used when hunting highly pressured puddle ducks as well as several species of sea duck in shallower salt marshes or tide pools.

One note: Many states have outlawed this type of structure. Be sure the state that's being hunted allows it.

Layout Blind

If you prefer using a manufactured style, there are many on the market. For the waterfowler who spends the bulk of his or her time lying among decoys, layout blinds are perfect. A layout blind allows you to stay completely concealed by two flaps of material, while you lie on your back. A great choice is the Avery Finisher Blind. This model is similar to lying in a chaise longue. If digging a pit isn't legal in your area, a layout blind is the only other suitable alternative.

Boat Blind

For the hunter who mostly hunts over water, boat blinds are a huge asset. Requiring both an inner frame and outer blind material, they are relatively simple to install and use. The hunter is totally concealed, but also afforded the benefit of quickly moving if the birds change their pattern. The sides are movable and swing out of your way when taking a shot. These blinds are available in many different camouflage patterns, but from experience, I have found the actual grass mats to be most effective. Secured to the frame like any other blind material, the grass or raffia resembles natural swamp grass or cattails more effectively than a standard netting.

BOATS

After calls and guns, boats are the next most important component of a waterfowler's arsenal. Depending on the species pursued, a hunter's choice of boat size and style is made easy. Here is a list of common styles:

Deep-V

The largest and most common size craft, the deep-V is able to endure the roughest water and harshest conditions. With its V-shaped hull, it's the tallest, ranging in widths from 10 feet (3 m) to more than 20 feet (6 m). With its size, it's able to carry heavier loads and several people. Most hunters use this style, with an outboard engine, to hunt larger water bodies. Medium to large outboards safely fit on most deep-V models. Although made mostly of aluminum and fiberglass, some wooden models are still in use.

Jon Boat

The jon boat is popular among multi-season hunters. Its hull is perfectly flat, easily able to float in shallow water. With high and stable sides, the jon can safely endure moderate waves and wind. Another appealing feature is its ability to safely carry large payloads and, depending on its length, two or three adults. Similar in durability to the deep-V, a medium-size outboard can be attached to the jon's transom for added speed. Jon boats are usually made of aluminum, but some are wood or fiberglass.

Canoe

One of the lightest vessels used today, the canoe is not only extremely quiet and stealthy, but also very agile. Due to its sleek and shallow design, a canoe can place hunters in swamps and cattail sloughs only a few inches (cm) deep. Employing identically shaped bow and stern, they are easily maneuverable among cattails and swamp grass. Canoes also are excellent choices when hauling gear behind another vessel. Canoes are commonly made of aluminum and fiberglass.

Layout Boat

Used primarily for hunting diver species on larger water bodies, these boats are commonly made of fiberglass and have a very low profile. Used by hunters who are trying to blend in among rafts of decoys, they sit extremely low in the water, and are usually painted black or dark blue, which also helps them blend in with the surface of the water. Another way they better blend into the surroundings is having no transom. Consequently, they must be towed to the hunting area by another vessel. Those boats are commonly built for a single hunter, though double versions do exist.

Sculling Boat

Similar in design to a layout vessel, the sculling boat is a two-person craft designed to be propelled by the rear person who rows an oar through a single hole in the transom. When jump-shooting flocked or rafting birds, the shooter sits in the front of the craft and waits until the flock is within shooting range. This style is very effective when hunting non-pressured diver species and geese. Due to its steering and propelling system, there is no room for an engine. Sculling boats are usually crafted of fiberglass.

OTHER HUNTING METHODS

Calling and decoying waterfowl may be two of the most exciting ways to harvest birds. Nonetheless, there are many different techniques sportsmen use when these methods aren't successful. The use of supplemental techniques is dictated by the particular circumstances. Quite often it's simply not feasible for a hunter to create a lifelike spread. It may be because the birds are too spread-shy to offer a clean shot, or because of poor topography. Having at least a couple alternative strategies available can salvage a hunt. Here are a few options:

Pass-Shooting

To understand pass-shooting, think of passing a ball on a soccer field. One hunter pushes the birds down the line, another hunter joins in, and eventually the birds reach the goal.

Pass-shooting involves posting a waterfowler in an area where ducks frequently fly from point A to point B, with hopes that they will fly within range. This method is hugely popular when hunting narrow creeks or in heavy-pressure scenarios where birds are commonly flying. A hunter's patience and shooting skill are often tested, as ranges can fluctuate from 10 to 50 yards (9 to 45.5 m). Birds could be flying with the wind or against it and, unlike as in calling and decoying, the birds won't usually give you a second chance.

Important to remember is the constantly changing lead you must calculate. Unlike decoying, these birds are flying past you. Depending on wind, distance and shot type, the lead changes. Usually it's as simple as shooting for the bill when birds are less than 15 yards (13.6 m) away. The lead becomes 4 to 5 inches (10 to 12.7 cm) at 20 to 30 yards (18.2 to 27.3 m), and 6 inches (15 cm) to more than a foot (30 cm) past 30 yards. Shots past 30 yards should be saved for the more experienced wingshooters, or passed up altogether to avoid cripples. There are sure to be other, closer targets if you are in position and concealed well.

Usually, hunting a highly pressured creek and cattail slough during the first few days every year, I have found pass-shooting to be the best means of consistently putting birds on the table. Most hunters employ some form of decoy and calling, but their actual shooting is usually minimal. Use your knowledge of the surrounding water bodies that are also being hunted, then locate key topographical features—points, small bays, etc.—and simply stand there until birds fly by. While this method can be slow, it's usually quite productive, as the ducks are driven from the larger water by the other gunners and back into the setbacks—right where you are!

Another example of effective pass-shooting is to locate a roosted flock of ducks or geese and slip in between them and their morning route, before daylight. For this tactic to bring success, you must know the direction the geese will travel. Usually they use a specific field during a specific period. Knowing the direction of their morning travels will continually put you in the correct position. If you are lucky enough to locate a cattail or grassy edge between the birds and their destination, all the better. You can stealthily wait for the geese to pass overhead. This is a tactic that works well, especially for novice hunters. For the hunter who doesn't want to carry huge decoy spreads, or prefers to be mobile, pass-shooting is the answer.

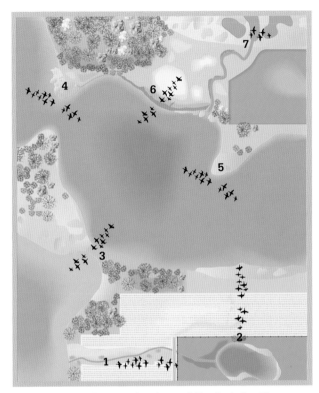

Prime locations for pass-shooting puddlers include: (1) stream corridors, (2) feeding fields between lakes or potholes, (3) passes between refuges and public waters, (4) narrows between two lake basins, (5) major points, (6) steep hills along the water's edge and (7) emergent vegetation around a cluster of sloughs.

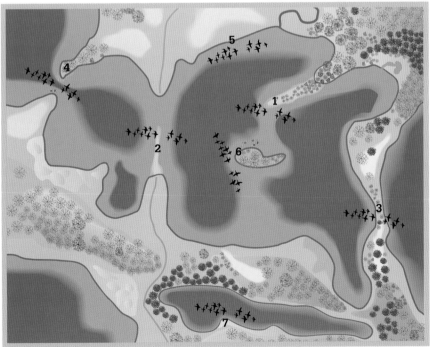

Prime locations for pass-shooting divers include: (1) major points, (2) flooded roadbeds or old railroad crossings, (3) passes between two bodies of water, (4) a narrows between two lakes, (5) long, straight shorelines (on windy days), (6) islands and (7) points on smaller adjacent lakes.

Jump-Shooting

Another method used by hunters who prefer fast action is jump-shooting. Made popular by hunters who were used to jumping grouse and other upland birds, jump-shooting requires very fast reflexes and keen eyesight. It's the hunter's goal to see the birds before they jump. Utilizing common still-hunting techniques as with hunting deer or other big game, the jump-shooter silently slips through flooded timber or grassy creeks, or along a field edge or pothole swamp. Jump-shooting can also be done from a boat or canoe, but many states don't allow shooting from a moving boat. So make sure the craft is stopped before actually taking the shot.

Occasionally, birds may lift early. If this happens, you must quickly decide if the shot is safe. Preferably, the birds are spotted first. To raise the birds, a yell or clap usually does the trick to jump them. If the birds instead try to slip away into the reeds, you may want to fire a shot at a swimmer to raise the rest. Usually, a shot in the air will also raise them, but this can be a difficult choice if you are using a single shot rather than a double-barrel.

Unlike pass-shooting, leading birds while jump-shooting isn't an issue. Knowing the area and flight patterns of the birds, the experienced jump-shooter should be able to get well within range before spooking them. On average, shots range from about 15 to 30 yards (13.6 to 27.3 m), and knowing puddle ducks to be able to rise straight into the air, shots are at a rising target.

Remember, all shots should be aimed toward the head, as the birds are constantly gaining altitude, and shots at the body are sure to miss or cripple. If you find yourself shooting at passing birds or at birds that have already traveled a good distance from the original jumping point, it's best to reevaluate your approach.

While the brunt of jump-shooting is done when pursuing geese or puddle species, divers can also be taken with this strategy. This almost always requires using a boat and shooting at flying birds.

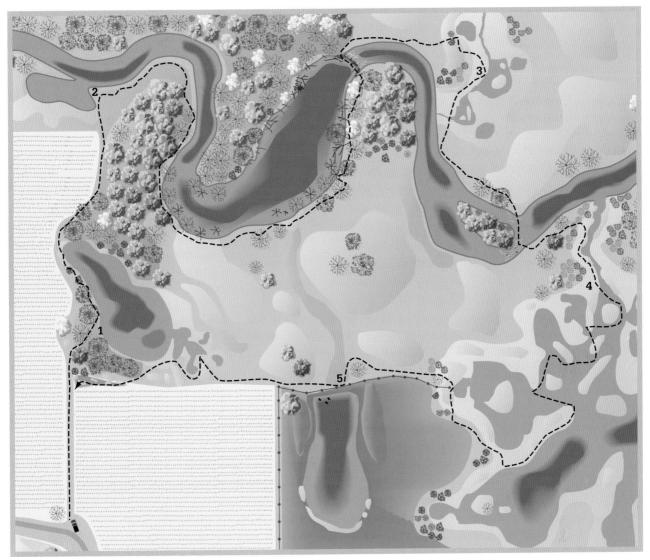

A good idea is to plan a "milk run" that will take you to several good jump-shooting locations and return you to your starting point without backtracking. In this example, you park on a gravel road and (1) walk into a small pothole near a grain field. From there, you (2) follow the course of a winding stream, (3) check a small connecting slough, (4) move on to a shallow marshy area and (5) sneak up on a stock tank where ducks were spotted from a distance. Then you return to the starting point.

Driving

Similar to driving deer or pheasants, duck and goose drives are formed by placing as many as ten, or more, hunters behind the flock, with "sitters" or ambushers in position to shoot when the birds pass by. Sometimes used for hunting puddlers, driving is predominantly done by goose and diver hunters. Because both these waterfowl species either rest in the middle of fields or raft far from cover, drives work well for these stationary scenarios.

When jumping birds from water, two or more boats are needed for the drivers. The ambushers use a low-profile layout or "sneak" boat, and scull slowly toward the flock while the others move faster to lift them. Or, the shooters wait perfectly still for the birds to pass in front or overhead.

Always remember to check local game laws before attempting any drive or push, as some states don't allow driving waterfowl.

Treestand Hunting

If you ask most experienced waterfowlers whether treestands can be used in taking birds, they would probably laugh and walk away. The idea that tree stands would ever be necessary is far from their thinking. But within the past few years I have found the use of treestands to be a huge advantage!

Bow hunting a few years ago, I was perched on the edge of a cornfield over a well-used afternoon deer trail. Knowing that not only deer, but turkeys and many species of waterfowl, were using the field, I would regularly see many birds feeding on the excess corn. Watching a flock of Canada geese fly over the same ridge every evening to feed in the middle of the cornfield, it occurred to me that it was quite possible for a hunter to harvest geese on a regular basis by simply standing on the ridge. With goose season rapidly approaching, I planned to do just that on the first evening.

Arriving on the ridge several evenings later, this time with a 12-gauge, I settled in and waited for the birds to arrive. Like clockwork they appeared, but because of the foliage, they were hardly visible. It was from this experience that I learned to either climb the tree or, better yet, use a stand to more safely wait for the birds. The following evening, I got my limit after only two flocks passed by.

Remembering the science behind flight patterns and natural topography, it's now blindingly apparent why the geese were using that ridge and, consequently, why I was so successful. It only takes a few days of shooting to shove the flock either right or left. Continually moving a stand ensures success.

Although geese are the most common waterfowl species that can be harvested through these means, mallards, blacks and woodies are also susceptible to this tactic. One reason is that they regularly feed on farm crops as well as acorns. In some instances when ducks are feeding on the ridges, you can create a combination jump-shoot/tree-stand hunt all in one evening.

TREE HUNTING TIPS

Here are a few tips for hunting from a tree:

- First and foremost, wear a safety belt or harness at all times.

- Shot requirements are slightly different from traditional waterfowling because shots are usually through at least a light canopy layer. And because these are big birds, I recommend using Hevi-Shot only. Shot size should range from 2s to BBB, or even T.

- 12-gauge 3½-inch (8.9-cm) magnums and 10-gauges are excellent choices.

- Bring a small fishing rod for retrieving birds. Often both ducks and geese fall into the crotch of a tree or branch. You may need a way of shaking dead birds from these crevices. An appropriate line pound-test is anything 20 (9 kg) or larger. Large spoons with giant treble hooks work well for securing the bird to the line.

USING HUNTING DOGS

For many, waterfowling is held dear because of the camaraderie and pleasure of hunting with a well-trained retriever. An obedient water dog is also a valuable tool. It's been documented that a quarter of all ducks that are downed are never recovered. The percentage drops dramatically with the use of a dog. This is reason enough for the conscientious and conservation-minded waterfowler to have a good dog on the hunt.

When choosing a dog, it's important to ask questions about bloodlines. For example, common to Labradors is amateur owners breeding their animals with inferior mates. Consequently, bloodlines become tainted and health issues such as heart problems, hip displasia and conditions associated with exposure to loud noises are common. Relying on a reputable breeder usually avoids these issues, and if a problem dog is obtained, the breeder usually provides a replacement.

There are a multitude of species available to the duck and goose hunter, including labs, chessies, goldens and even wire-hairs. They all can do the job; your decision may be based on anything from researching genetic information to a simple personal preference.

Labrador Retriever

The most common choice is a Labrador breed—black, yellow or chocolate color phase. Don't believe any of those old wives' tales that unfairly label certain colors as harder to train, lazy or downright ignorant. In reality, all color phases are equally intelligent and ambitious.

One benefit to owning one of the Labrador breeds is its ability to endure icy water and cold air temperatures. For many northern shooters, this can mean the difference between hunting only the early season or throughout the migration period. Other benefits include having a strong nose, making an excellent house dog and having the ability to learn upland hunting tactics.

The overall size of labs can fluctuate from bloodline to bloodline, but the average weight is around 70 pounds (31.5 kg). The largest lab I ever owned was a male chocolate that topped the scales at 105 pounds (47 kg)!

Chesapeake Bay Retriever

Closely related to the lab is the "chessie," an excellent cold-weather animal. Tolerant of late-season conditions, they have no qualms about hunting to the end of the season. Some breeders believe that this breed is difficult to train. From my experience, this isn't the case, and they also make good pets.

It's also an excellent upland flushing breed.

Golden Retriever

Another excellent breed for waterfowling, the golden has, on average, a softer temperament than most labs. One disadvantage to the golden lies in its coat. Much longer and feathery in comparison to a lab's coat, the golden's coat lacks insulating capacity. It is also much more difficult to dry. Unfortunately, goldens usually dislike icy or colder conditions. The golden averages 70 pounds (31.5 kg) in weight.

German Wire-Haired Pointer

Least common among owners of waterdogs is the wire-hair. Used more often to hunt upland species, it is only a fair retriever. These dogs are small in comparison, averaging about 55 to 60 pounds (25 to 27 kg).

CHAPTER TEN

Shotguns and Ammunition

With recent technological advances, the days of simplicity are now past. The time when sportsmen simply chose between the reliable pump action and the faster semi-automatic shotgun are gone. Hunters now have many more gun choices, plus the opportunity to customize and/or invest in a better-functioning and often beautiful piece. Hotter gun powders, cutting-edge shot types, and the addition of the 3½-inch (8.9-cm) chamber, has added a new dimension to waterfowling.

The top three most popular styles of wingshooting shotgun remain the break-open double-barrel, the pump action, and the semi-automatic. And with each usually chambered in the hard-hitting 12-gauge version, the choice can still seem simple. On the other hand, a plethora of both cosmetic and mechanical choices await you.

CHOOSING A SHOTGUN

First in choosing the proper waterfowling weapon, selection should be based on its principal use. For many sportsmen the functionality of a semi-automatic is preferred, as it affords more shots at a swifter pace. Chambered in standard 12-gauge, it gives the average hunter the flexibility to either shoot the lower-powered 2¾- or 3-inch (7- or 7.6-cm) magnum shells. These two chamber-length options afford a versatile approach for the multi-season sportsman–from teal to geese, the multi-season hunter can carry both shell sizes and load accordingly.

Many sportsmen opt for the slightly larger 3½-inch chamber capacity. Offering more pellets per shell, being harder hitting, and having longer down-range killing power, these shells offer the needed inertia when chasing larger or down-range birds. Of course, 3½-inch shells aren't for everyone. When pursuing smaller duck species, this size can be unnecessary. The majority of duck hunters today rely heavily on the 3-inch.

Semi-automatic (top), pump (middle), double-barrel (bottom).

In a nutshell, here are your three basic shotgun options:

- **Semi-automatic.** Each pull of the trigger fires one shell, and another is automatically chambered. There are two basic types of semi-automatics: gas-operated and recoil-operated. The recoil type is very reliable, but tends to "kick" more. If you're using light loads, a recoil gun may not eject empty shells as well as a gas gun.

- **Pump.** Sliding the fore-end back and forth ejects a spent shell and chambers another one. With a little practice, you can shoot a pump just as fast and accurately as a semi-automatic.

- **Double-barrel.** To open the hinge action to insert or eject shells, you push a lever or button at the rear of the receiver. Double-barrels come in side-by-side or over-and-under models. A double has one big advantage over other actions: it gives you the option of selecting a different choke for each barrel.

Once you have decided on the general shotgun type and chamber size, you next need to decide on a brand and model. You can often get help with

this decision from the local sporting goods store or at the local gun club. Remember, this can be a life-long investment, so do the proper research. If possible, ask to shoot the gun before purchasing it. Many dealers now offer to let you "test shoot" guns at a local range. The additional time will be well worth the information you gain.

Once the brand and model has been purchased, many cosmetic and mechanical modifications can be made to better prepare for the coming seasons. Here are a few popular options:

- If the gun isn't camouflaged, a cloth gun snake can be fit over it. Made of a cotton-spandex, it simply fits over the gun, guarding against any unnecessary glare.

- The traditional method of camouflaging is still employed today: using camouflage tape on all shiny or metallic parts.

- Once the firearm blends in better with its natural surroundings, many sportsmen with poor vision often install fiber-optic beads or aiming apparatuses. Commonly, the original bead is simply replaced with a fiber-optic bead. For

Semi-automatic

Pump

shooters having difficulty finding the target and achieving a shot picture, a second bead can be added approximately at half the length of the barrel, which will force the shooter's head down onto the receiver, to achieve the needed shot picture.

- Some have added holographic sights, which are placed at the end of the receiver and create a larger site picture. While these can be effective, the initial learning curve can take some time, as stance and head-and-cheek positions are no longer important. You simply put the target in the viewfinder and pull the trigger, which really goes against the basics of shotgunning at first.

- Another easy and necessary modification is the addition of a sling. Slings can be crucial when initially carrying in gear, and later when carrying out birds. Many guns come standard with slings.

- Barrels can be bored and tapped by gunsmiths to fit today's common screw-in choke tubes. Quite often with older shotguns, the barrels were manufactured with a fixed choke. Today, either a barrel can be bored or tapped, or a new barrel can be purchased to give the hunter more choices.

Double-barrel

Choke Tube Selection

To prevent the shot from scattering too much, shotgun barrels must decrease in diameter at the muzzle. The amount of constriction, called the choke, determines the size and density of your shot pattern.

Open (wide) chokes, such as skeet and cylinder, are seldom used for duck hunting because they do not provide shot density adequate to kill a good-sized duck at normal shooting distances. Chokes most commonly used in duck hunting (from widest to narrowest) include: improved-cylinder, modified, improved-modified and full.

As a rule, the greater the expected shooting distance, the narrower the choke you should use. But when using a full-choke barrel, shot size is also a consideration. Most shotgun manufacturers advise against using steel shot larger than size 1 because abrasion from the hard shot may "blow out" the choke. Shooting large steel shot through a full choke may result in overconstriction and too many pellets that sail erratically and separate from the main shot group.

Waterfowlers used to march to their blinds with full chokes only. Coupled with the use of lead shot, it was a deadly combination. Today, with the ban on lead, sportsmen have reevaluated their choke choices.

While a full choke was fine for lead shot, it isn't acceptable for steel. With a consistency that's much harder and lighter, a choke with a supertight constriction is bound to disfigure steel shot, leaving gaps in the pattern. It also allows the pellets to bounce, creating an uneven or blotched pattern. With older, fixed-choke shotguns, it's not only ineffective to shoot a full choke, but over time it also damages the bore. With steel shot, the preferred choke is modified, as it affords just enough constriction to create a full-choke effect with the steel pellets.

But, that isn't the last word on shooting steel. Bird species, distance and shot size all play a role in deciding which choke to install in your weapon for a particular day.

The following three recommendations are for choosing the best choke when shooting steel shot. (When shooting other nontoxic hybrid shot, a full choke suffices in nearly all situations. If the shots are aimed at closer birds, an open pattern is necessary.)

- **Any Size Bird, Close Distance:** When hunting over decoys during the early season, when birds are far from wary, the larger, tighter payloads are not necessary. Even when decoying early-season geese, as long as the shots are 25 yards (22.75 m) or closer, a light-modified choke will work well. It allows a more open pattern, giving you more room for error. When hunting in close quarters, larger shot pellets won't be necessary, as the inertia at short distances is moot. Shot in sizes 7½ up to 5 work the best.

- **Medium Distance, Species Specific:** For many years, hunters believed that at distances between 25 and 35 yards (22.75 to 31.85 m), only a tighter-constricting modified choke would be sufficient for steel shooters. Today, thanks to much test patterning, it's been proven that for wood ducks and teal, a lighter-modified or even an improved-cylinder choke works well. They spread out the overall shot pattern, making close, quick shots much easier to accomplish. With larger birds, such as geese, a straight-modified choke is preferred, as it has more energy to cleanly harvest these tougher birds.

- **Larger Birds, Long Distances:** When hunting in pass-shooting situations or for high-flying targets, large numbers of pellets are necessary to cleanly dispatch a large bird. Where shots are longer than 35 to 40 yards (31.85 to 36.4 m) and pellet size is larger than 4, a standard, modified choke creates the needed constriction to reach and down the larger, farther birds.

Here are a few common shotgun options:

Remington's model 1187sps (special purpose semi-automatic), chambered in 12 gauge 2³/4- to 3¹/2-inch (7- to 8.9-cm), employs a 28-inch (71-cm) barrel, versus the 30-inch (76-cm) length of the 1100 mag. It's relatively light to carry at only 7¹/2 pounds (3.4 kg). The 1187sps comes with the Remington choke system, which includes improved-cylinder, modified and full chokes. It is available in Mossy Oak Break Up camo or in plain walnut. The 1187sps offers the versatility needed for a several-season year. From teal to greater Canadas, you're covered.

Another popular offering is the Mossberg Ultra-Mag pump. Chambered in 2³/4- to 3¹/2-inch lengths, it sports a 28-inch barrel and the Accu-Mag choke system. For younger hunters or individuals trying to avoid recoil, the Mossberg isn't a good choice—it's a pump model with no recoil-reducing gas chambers so it kicks like a mule. Costing much less than most waterfowling shotguns, this model continues to be popular with hunters on a budget—and with a strong shoulder.

Browning's BPS is a pump chambered the same as the Remington and the Mossberg. It's offered in four different barrel lengths: 24, 26, 28 and 30 inches (61, 66, 71, 76 cm) with the Invector choke system. Shot for shot, you will find the recoil is much less than that of the Mossberg, but more than that of the 1187sps.

Benelli's Nova pump has great versatility. It is chambered the same as the otherguns mentioned, and is offered in 24-, 26- and 28-inch barrel lengths. It is one of the only firearms that allows the chamber to open for ejecting the lead shell without emptying the magazine. However, by simply employing the pump (where the button is located), it may inadvertently eject the shell, and no other shell advances. This isn't an everyday occurrence, but common enough, that you may be frustrated when trying to fire multiple shots at decoying birds and only firing blanks after the first report.

Remington's SP semi-automatic 10 gauge is very popular with many hunters mainly pursuing geese or, where legal, cranes and swans. Weighing moe than 10 pounds (4.5 kg), it's quite an armful to carry, but manufactured with the Remington choke system, it is extremely deadly even beyond 60 yards (55 m) on larger birds. Despite the fact that it's a semiautomatic, it's quite the shoulder thumper.

SHOT TYPE AND SIZE OPTIONS

Until recently, lead ruled the globe. With its ban, steel became the replacement. Much less dense and very hard, big leads or fast shots were no longer as important because of steel's blazing speed out of the barrel. Choosing loads used to be a simple process; size was all that was relevant. Whatever size a shooter preferred in lead, the next size or two up in steel would suffice. For example, number 4s would be changed to size 2s or BBs. This very general example takes into consideration that the sportsman isn't planning any jump-shooting or close-decoying kills. If so, a higher pellet count found in the smaller sizes is usually preferred.

Since those earlier days, the market has been flooded with new and intriguing shot types and load styles. Steel no longer reigns. But don't mistake that for obsolescence; it remains the most popular shot type used today. It's extremely affordable and remains the fastest.

While much slower, yet denser and easier to pattern, the recent development of various nontoxics and their hybrids has changed the sport of waterfowling. The

three major types of non-toxic shot are bismuth, tungsten and Hevi-Shot. While these choices afford the waterfowler a more ethical choice and higher performance, they remain quite expensive.

• **Bismuth:** While superior to steel in almost all aspects, bismuth has a consistency which is very brittle. At just ten percent lighter than lead, it offers more down-range killing power than steel, but is apt to shatter, creating some patterning problems and issues when preparing game for the table. It's believed that choosing one size larger than the lead equivalent will suffice, but I have found little difference. It's recommended that the larger bismuth loads be shot through modified or light-full chokes. Leading should be fairly consistent with many steel loads.

• **Tungsten:** Much less brittle than bismuth, and only six percent lighter than lead, tungsten succeeds where bismuth leaves off. Given its more malleable properties, shattering isn't a problem and patterning is much easier. Shooting tungsten through a full choke is common, but the versatility of a modified choke is usually preferred. Unlike with steel, taking into consideration distance and speed is necessary when judging lead distance, as tungsten tends to be much slower. The hybrids of tungsten include the tungsten-polymer and tungsten-matrix.

• **Remington Hevi-Shot:** Fourteen percent denser than lead, and much softer, Hevi-Shot not only carries more down-range killing power than any other shot type, it also holds a world record for placing 42 pellets in a 3-inch (7.6 cm) circle at 40 yards (36.4 m). Hevi-Shot has no hard or brittle qualities, making it the best all-around choice for any waterfowler. Full chokes are used regularly for pass-shooting or when decoying large spreads. To date, it's the safest shot to fire from any modern shotgun as well as the hardest hitting.

Patterning

It's important to select a shell that matches a particular choke constriction, as well as one that's affordable. It's also important to know where the overall pattern is in relation to the target. As with sighting-in a big-game rifle, shotgunners must invest time and effort in examining the best pattern for their particular shotgun. The best way to get the most effective pattern is to purchase a box of several different shot types and sizes and fire your shotgun at differing yardages. Following is a good strategy to help you gain the information you need.

First, pace out a few yardages common to the waterfowling scenarios you will face—30, 40 and 50 yards (27, 36 and 45 m) are good choices. Prepare three paper targets with 30-inch (76 cm) "kill zone" circles. To save time, have a target and backdrop for each distance you test.

Next, choose one brand, shot type and size to fire at each of the three targets. You will probably find that certain brands pattern better at one yardage than at other yardages. After you have shot the first three, examine the results. Where is the majority of the pattern? Is it high? Is it low? Is it evenly distributed on the paper? Did you flinch? Does your shoulder hurt too much to accurately shoot the next selection? These are all good questions to answer.

If shot pellets seem scattered, it's possible that the choke is too constrictive. If the opposite is true, the pattern may be too tight for your planned effective close-range gunning. Continue your testing with a variety of shells and distances. It may take more than one session to finally determine the best shell for the distances you normally encounter, but this time spent will be well worth it.

CHAPTER ELEVEN

Clothing and Accessories

There are few sports where choice of clothing is as vital as with waterfowling. Dressing for success can be quite complicated when budgeting for the multiple waterfowl seasons. From cotton tees to wool to Gore-Tex, the prepared hunter needs a varied wardrobe to ensure comfort. Historically, tweed or tan cotton-duck bird jackets were the standard. Today, sportsmen also hunt many climates, which consequently demands even more variety. Thanks to manufacturers with a wide range of offerings, hunters easily find the quality and variety they need.

Early Season

In late August and September, gunning can consist of early wood duck hunts, teal shoots and resident Canada goose hunting opportunities. Hunters are forced to lie in arid fields one moment, and then huddle along debris in a muggy marsh the next. Temperatures and weather can change in a heartbeat, making clothing choice difficult. During these early periods, it's best to be as versatile as possible.

For the budget-conscious hunter, long-sleeved cotton T-shirts coupled with sweat pants is a great choice for hotter, drier conditions. This combination is affordable for having several sets in different camouflage patterns. I usually have two sets, one for hunting around small potholes and grass, and one for lying among decoys in lush, green fields.

Another option for when the sun is high is to wear a short-sleeved T-shirt and shorts, and apply camouflage makeup to mask any naked skin. When hunting the first few days of the early teal season, I have found this technique invaluable to help overcome the usual higher temperatures.

Mid-Season

When temperatures dip or precipitation is falling, a different approach to clothing is necessary. In most of the country, the last weeks in September through the first couple weeks in October can leave hunters wishing they had prepared better. On any given day, morning temperatures can hover around 40°F (4.4°C) or less and then rise to 60°F (15.5°C) or more. Waterfowlers seem prone to dress for one period of the day, but somehow forget to prepare for other weather conditions. This is when light layering with breathable clothing is best. Wicking moisture away from the skin, while securing stored air for warmth, is one of the secrets to continued comfort. Along with light layering, the benefits of a breathable material make clothing selection easier.

Manufacturers, such as Browning, Cabela's, Columbia, Dupont, Gore-Tex and Quaker Boy, offer excellent clothing systems to meet the needs of any hunting scenario.

Here are some things to keep in mind when selecting a parka:

- **Durability.** The shell should be made of tough, long-lasting material such as tightly woven nylon.

- **Camouflage.** Select the camo pattern that best matches the cover in which you'll be hunting. Some coats are reversible, giving you the option of two different camo patterns.

- **Water Repellency.** The shell should be waterproof or have a breathable waterproof liner to protect you against rain, snow or splashing waves. Breathable shells are more expensive, but prevent perspiration buildup.

- **Liner.** Many parkas come with a zip-out liner that can be quickly removed for hunting in warm weather. Or, you can wear the liner but not the shell. This adds great versatility to your hunting outfit.

- **Pockets.** A good parka has plenty of pockets for shells, gloves, extra calls and other accessories.

Waterfowling pants are available in insulated or uninsulated models. They usually have a tough nylon camo shell and a liner of Gore-Tex or other breathable material. Some hunters prefer pants to bibs, because they're less bulky and more comfortable. But they may not be warm enough in very cold weather. Some lightweight pants can be worn inside waders.

If you'll be hunting in waders, you need a jacket short enough that it won't get wet. An elastic band along the bottom helps keep the jacket snug at the waist to prevent a draft. A wading jacket should have the same features as a good parka.

If you're not using waders, you'll want insulated, waterproof camo bibs that extend up to chest level. Be sure the legs have zippers long enough that you can easily slip the bibs over your boots. In mild weather, you can wear bibs with only a camo shirt; in cold weather, under a parka. Bibs are usually made from the same materials as parkas.

Waders or hip boots are a necessity for most types of duck hunting. Even if you're hunting on land, they'll keep you from getting wet and muddy. Be sure they fit tightly at the ankle; otherwise, they'll pull off easily when you're walking in muck. Most duck hunters prefer boot-foot to stocking-foot waders, because the shoes that fit over the latter type tend to fill with mud and debris. Always wear a well-tightened belt around the waist of your waders. This way, they won't completely fill with water should you wade too deep or fall in.

Late Season

Layering with breathable fabrics such as Gore-Tex is the key to warm, non-clammy comfort. The late-season hunter uses the same concepts when choosing proper cold-weather clothing, as those hunting months range from December through February.

While it wasn't necessary for early- and mid-season wardrobes to include insulated full-length underwear, it's now imperative that some form of under insulation be worn, preferably in a heavier weight. Temperatures on average will hover around freezing and below. Long underwear in heavier thicknesses and weights is necessary to catch and store the needed body heat for sustained warmth.

Unprepared shooters may embark with only the bare-waffle-knit style. This is a major mistake! While it may have been sufficient for slowly still-hunting for deer just a month before, its design doesn't work for sitting perfectly still for extended periods of time duck or goose hunting. Only fleece or heavy silk types will do.

Once you have selected the proper underwear, adding layers and sub-layers is necessary to ward off wind and cold. Beginning with socks, it's important to wick away any moisture that collects, especially if the day's endeavors include wearing waders. The best formula for dry and warm feet is wearing two pairs of socks.

First, a regular cotton pair of casual socks wicks moisture away from the skin, and then a warmer pair of wool or polar-fleece socks acts as further insulation. For the hunter who wants to use his or her regular non-waterproof, cold-weather footwear, adding a pair of waterproof socks is the ticket.

Layering for the legs is also very important. Manufacturers offer pants that incorporate the thickness and warmth of fleece, while also utilizing technology to ensure complete dryness. The final, outer layer for the legs depends on the day's plans. If open water is still present, then a pair of chest waders is necessary.

Choosing any cold-weather wader is relatively simple if two major qualifications are met. First, they must be made of neoprene. Second, the neoprene thickness can be no less than 5 mm. While hunting waders are regularly manufactured in 3 mm, they simply aren't warm enough.

Because a person's trunk truly is the heating core for the entire body, you must layer heavily to minimize heat loss. For long-underwear tops, layers should be somewhat loose and non-binding or the heat storing action of the air pockets will be reduced. Any loose fleece pullover is a great choice to ensure air trapping. Next, another loose-fitting fleece or windproof pullover on top of the first fleece is key to long-term insulation. Lastly, wearing a parka completes an effective upper-body system for warmth.

Gloves, Mittens and Muffs

Your personal preference and needs determine what hand gear, if any, you wear while hunting. The simple cotton-jersey-style gloves come in many camouflage patterns, and work great to camouflage your hands. When shooting in cooler weather, they also help insulate under a heavier pair.

Two types of gloves that most waterfowlers can't live without are: the elbow-length decoy gloves and a pair of insulated shooting gloves.

Many younger shooters, who aren't yet bothered by arthritis or poor circulation, prefer the mobility of a muff over any encumbering mittens or gloves. Simply strapped to their waist, a muff is very handy.

Of course, you may opt to wear nothing at all on your hands. This certainly gives you complete freedom of your hands and fingers.

Hats

Probably, personal preference and sentimental reasoning put more hats on heads than temperature and weather combined. How often have you launched your duck boat during a cold wintry morning, only to see a hunter wearing an old, torn and faded boonie hat? It doesn't repel water, insulate or even fit anymore. But he has grown attached to it, and with it, the luck he's sure it brings him. While I'm not suggesting trashing every sportsman's favorite lucky hat, here is a list of some options available, if you should decide to trade up.

• **Gore-Tex Jones Cap.** Probably the most commonly used today, it is one of my personal favorites. Designed with a scoop brim around the entire circumference of the cap and a Gore-Tex lining, it is completely waterproof and breathable. Another added feature are the slide-down ear flaps that can be quickly pulled into place when needed.

• **Baseball-Style Cap.** Initially designed to reduce glare and camouflage the head, these are now offered with a Gore-Tex lining to make them waterproof. Due to their design, they aren't as protective as the Jones cap, but are more comfortable during warm weather.

• **Yazoo.** Wearing this style through years of beaver trapping and ice fishing has shown me its insulating ability. Available in many camouflage patterns, these hats will not only camouflage the majority of the face with their pull-down cheek flaps, but also keep you warm. Many are also 100-percent waterproof.

Neck Warmers and Facemasks

Available in cotton or polar fleece, neck warmers are chosen by many hunters. I almost always utilize some form of facemask. Originally used by turkey hunters, facemasks quickly caught on among waterfowl hunters. The ability to not only look at oncoming flocks, but to be able to watch and gauge their body language while calling and not worry about any facial glare is priceless.

For cooler waterfowling weather, fleece facemasks are offered with corresponding headwear, including baseball-cap style, bucket hat and convertible-dome caps. Much warmer than the mesh styles, the fleece is guaranteed to keep even the coldest mug warm.

Footwear

For waterfowl hunting you might want to consider neoprene waders for warm-, cool- or cold-weather hunting (you can also buy rubber waders, which are less expensive, and fabric-coated rubber waders, in which the rubber is sandwiched between two layers of canvas or Cordura, for extra durability). Hip boots also come in fabric-coated rubber, neoprene and rubber models. Leather boots are for warm-weather hunting on dry land and felt-lined pac boots are for late-season, cold-weather hunting.

In very cold weather, when much of the water has frozen up, felt pacs make the best footwear. The rubber bottoms allow you to walk in some water and the thick insulation keeps your feet warm even when you're sitting in a blind for hours.

Waterfowling Accessories

As with any other hands-on sport or activity, you need a dependable base of gear to get started. Aside from decoys, calls, shotguns and boats, there are many behind-the-scenes tools and accessories that can make any trip more enjoyable and successful. Of course, don't forget to bring enough food and water to keep everyone in the group happy and comfortable. A first-aid kit is also a good idea. Here are a few more options to consider:

• **Portable Heater.** An excellent companion in the duck blind or goose pit. These can burn either kerosene or propane, depending on the model, and are sure to pay for themselves the first day they are used. Along with keeping everyone warm, they also can be used to reheat coffee or cook breakfast.

• **Flashlight.** Almost too obvious to mention, but this tool is too often forgotten at home.

• **Bucket or Milk Crate.** Not missed if you are wearing waders, but if you have no other kind of waterproof protection, this can avoid a cold rear!

• **GPS.** Useful whether hunting on large water, in flooded timber or fog, for example, if you find yourself turned around and need help getting back to camp.

• **CB Radio/Cell Phone.** Other options for staying connected, especially when hunting larger lakes or the open sea. Also useful for calling for help in an emergency.

• **Waterproof "Dry" Bag.** Sometimes called "blind" bags, they are an excellent investment for carrying extras, such as an extra parka or shells—or a couple sandwiches.

• **Hearing Assistance.** Using products like Walker's Game Ear can make the difference between being ready and missing a shot opportunity.

Afterword

As little as a century ago, waterfowl populations weren't nearly as plentiful as they are today. Small to no bag limits, coupled with a huge market for feathers and meat, and the complexities of a troubling economy, sent every able-bodied hunter in search of an exciting and lucrative trade.

To be expected, by 1934, North American waterfowl populations reached a devastatingly low level. At approximately 27 million birds overall, over-hunting and the destruction of wetlands was taking its toll. Some species, such as the wood duck, were recorded as nearing extinction.

Fearing that tragic end for more species, J. N. "Ding" Darling, the chief of the U.S. Biological Survey (now United States Fish and Wildlife Service) implemented a management strategy mandating that all waterfowl hunters purchase a federal duck stamp. He hoped this conservation stamp would give the government much needed funding to purchase future wetland and grassland habitats, which are crucial for breeding and nesting activities.

Today, Ding's hopes have materialized. The 1934 Bird Hunting Stamp Act (commonly known as the "Duck Stamp Act") has aided in the purchase of over 500 million acres of habitat, with ninety percent of the proceeds being used for the betterment of waterfowl.

We present-day waterfowlers are very lucky that such an early and necessary step was taken on behalf of our sport. With continued support and a focused conservation effort, waterfowl numbers will prosper.

Resources

Aero Outdoors
509-545-8000
www.aerooutdoors.com

Alumacraft Boats
507-931-1050
870-246-5555
www.alumacraft.com

Avery Outdoors, Inc.
901-324-1500
www.averyoutdoors.com

Benelli USA
301-283-6981
www.benelliusa.com

Bobcat Boats, Inc.
866-933-8183
www.bobcatboats.com

Browning
800-333-3288
www.browning.com

Buck Gardner Calls
901-946-8747 (TN)
www.buckgardner.com

Cabela's
800-237-4444
www.cabelas.com

Carlson Championship Calls, LLC
402-554-8411
www.carlsoncalls.com

Cass Creek International, LLC
800-778-0389
www.casscreek.com

Columbia Sportswear
Company
503-985-4000
www.columbia.com

D&MB Blinds
218-855-0939
www.dmbblinds.com

Delta Waterfowl
888-987-3695
877-667-5656
www.deltawaterfowl.org

Devastator Game Calls
866-338-4868
www.devcalls.com

DJ Illinois River Valley
866-DJC-ALLS
www.djcalls.com

Drake Waterfowl Systems
662-895-3651
www.drakewaterfowl.com

Duck Blinds Unlimited
800-257-8979
www.duckblindsunlimited

Duck Commander Company
www.duckcommander.com

Ducks Unlimited, Inc.
800-45DUCKS
www.ducks.org

Echo Calls
501-882-2026
www.echocalls.com

Edge Expedite
715-381-2935
www.edgebyexpedite.com

Federal Cartridge Co.
800-322-2342
www.federalcartridge.com

Flagman Products
507-367-4782
www.flagmanproducts.com

Flambeau Outdoors
800-232-3474
www.flambeau.com

Flyways Specialties
229-226-5011
www.flywaysspecialties.com

Go Devil Duck Boats
888-490-3254
www.godevil.com

GooseView Industries
218-326-6332
www.gooseview.com

Gore-Tex Outerwear
800-431-GORE
www.gore-tex.com

Hancock's Advanced Outdoor
Products
509-522-0964

Haydel's Game Calls, Inc.
318-746-3586
www.haydels.com

Higdon Decoys, Inc.
270-443-8739
www.higdondecoys.com

Hunter's Specialties
319-395-0321 (IA)
www.hunterspec.com

Hunter's View
309-690-0000
www.huntersview.com

Knight & Hale Game Calls
479-782-8971
www.knightandhale.com

Last Look Outdoors, Inc.
www.lastlookdecoy.com

McAlister Company
662-349-9396
www.mcalisterclothing.com

Mojo Decoys
318-283-7777
www.mojodecoys.net

Mossy Oak
662-494-8859
www.mossyoak.com

National Shooting Sports
Foundation
www.nssf.org

North American Gamebird
Association
www.naga.org

O. F. Mossberg & Sons, Inc.
203-230-5300
www.mossberg.com

Open Zone, Inc.
626-573-9710
www.openzone2000.com

Outlaw Decoys
877-754-3345
www.outlaw.com

Penn's Woods Game Calls
724-468-8311
www.pennswoods.com

Performance Calls
651-983-9514
www.performancecalls.com

Primos Hunting Calls
601-879-9323 or 800-523-2395
www.primos.com

Quaker Boy Game Calls
800-544-1600
www.quakerboygamecalls.com

Realtree Camo
www.realtree.com

Remington Arms Company, Inc
800-243-9700
www.remington.com

Renzo's Decoys
800-583-5416
www.renzosdecoys.com

Rich-N-Tone
888-768-2255
www.richntone.com

Riverside Products, Inc.
870-818-7194
501-882-5541
www.duckcoffin.com

RoboDuk Mfg.
877-525-9571
www.roboduk.com

Roy Rhodes Championship Calls
937-698-7697
www.royrhodes.com

Sean Mann Outdoors
1-800-345-4539
www.seanmannoutdoors.com

Southern Game Calls
662-627-1967
www.southerngamecalls.com

State Waterfowl
Associations
Check with your state's DNR
web site

Stearns Manufacturing
Company
1-800-333-1179
www.stearnsinc.com

TurboJet Duck Decoys
www.turbojetdecoys.com

Ultimate Hunter Decoys
660-562-3838
www.ambushlures.com

Walker's Game Ear
800-424-1069
www.walkersgameear.com

Western Rivers
731-967-0987
www.western-rivers.com

Wiley Outdoor Products, Inc.
662-324-9188 (MS)
www.wileyoutdoorproducts.com

Wing Wavers, Inc.
866-WING-WVR
www.wingwavers.com

Wrangler Boat Company
330-854-6049
www.wranglerboats.com

Zink Calls
937-832-3436
www.zinkcalls.com

Index

Contributing Photographers

(Note: T=Top, C=Center, L=Left, R=Right)

Tricia Bergstue
Falconer, NY
© Tricia Bergstue: pp. 3(L, R), 121

John R. Ford
Thorp, WI
© John R. Ford: pp. 16(L), 18(R), 20(L), 23(Both), 24(R), 28(R), 36(L), 46(L), 49(L), 84(R)

Michael H. Francis
Billings, MT
© Michael H. Francis: pp. 10(B), 12, 17(R), 18(L), 22, 32(R), 34(R), 39(R), 42(B), 84(TL)

Michael Furtman
Duluth, MN
© MichaelFurtman.com: pp. 8(R), 9, 10(T), 11(B), 13(C), 14, 26, 28(L), 31(Both), 72, 83(T), 85(R), 100(B), 105(T), Back Cover(T)

Eric J. Hansen
Corvallis, OR
© Eric J. Hansen: pp. 11(T), 20(R), 21(R), 24(L), 30(R), 39(L), 46(R), 48(R)

Donald M. Jones
Troy, MI
© Donald M. Jones: pp. 8(BL), 13(T), 17(L), 25, 30(L), 34(L), 37(Both), 47(Both), 85(C), 89(Both), 91(TR), 94(T), 111(R)

Gary Kramer
Willows, CA
© GaryKramer.net: pp. 19, 33(Both), 35, 38(Both), 40(Both), 41(Both), 42(T), 43(Both), 49(R), 105(C)

William H. Mullins
Boise, ID
© William H. Mullins: pp. 6, 8(TL), 13(B), 21(L), 29(Both), 36(R), 48(L), 68, 69, 85(L)

Dusan Smetana
www.DusanSmetana.com
© Dusan Smetana: pp. 16(R), 50, 57(L), 60, 61(BL), 74, 77(Both), 81, 90, 91(CR), 94(B), 96(B), 98(B), 99(T), 105(B), 106, 112(T)

Will Smith
Bomoseen, VT
© Will Smith: pp. 3(C), 57(R), 64

Bill Vinje
Minot, ND
© Bill Vinje: pp. 32(L), 44, 82(B), 102(T)

Creative Publishing international
Your Complete Source of How-to Information for the Outdoors

Hunting Books
- Advanced Turkey Hunting
- Advanced Whitetail Hunting
- Bowhunting Equipment & Skills
- Bowhunter's Guide to Accurate Shooting
- The Complete Guide to Hunting
- Dog Training
- Duck Hunting
- Elk Hunting
- How to Think Like a Survivor
- Hunting Record-Book Bucks
- Mule Deer Hunting
- Muzzleloading
- Outdoor Guide to Using Your GPS
- Pronghorn Hunting
- Whitetail Hunting
- Whitetail Techniques & Tactics
- Wild Turkey

Fishing Books
- Advanced Bass Fishing
- The Art of Freshwater Fishing
- The Complete Guide to Freshwater Fishing

- Fishing for Catfish
- Fishing Rivers & Streams
- Fishing Tips & Tricks
- Fishing with Artificial Lures
- Inshore Salt Water Fishing
- Kids Gone Fishin'
- Largemouth Bass
- Live Bait Fishing
- Modern Methods of Ice Fishing
- Northern Pike & Muskie
- Offshore Salt Water Fishing
- Panfish
- Salt Water Fishing Tactics
- Smallmouth Bass
- Striped Bass Fishing: Salt Water Strategies
- Successful Walleye Fishing
- Trout
- Ultralight Fishing

Fly Fishing Books
- The Art of Fly Tying
- The Art of Fly Tying – CD ROM
- Complete Photo Guide to Fly Fishing

- Complete Photo Guide to Fly Tying
- Fishing Dry Flies
- Fishing Nymphs, Wet Flies & Streamers
- Fly-Fishing Equipment & Skills
- Fly Fishing for Beginners
- Fly Fishing for Trout in Streams
- Fly-Tying Techniques & Patterns

Cookbooks
- All-Time Favorite Game Bird Recipes
- America's Favorite Fish Recipes
- America's Favorite Wild Game Recipes
- Babe & Kris Winkelman's Great Fish & Game Recipes
- Backyard Grilling
- Cooking Wild in Kate's Camp
- Cooking Wild in Kate's Kitchen
- Dressing & Cooking Wild Game
- The New Cleaning & Cooking Fish
- Preparing Fish & Wild Game
- The Saltwater Cookbook
- Venison Cookery

To purchase these or other Creative Publishing international titles,
contact your local bookseller, or visit our website at
www.creativepub.com

The Complete
FLY FISHERMAN™